FROM INVISIBLE TO VALUABLE:
Skills for Career Success

Stories and practical steps for teens and young adults
to master the skills no one teaches you
but everyone expects you to know

Doron Noyman

Copyright © 2025 Doron Noyman. All rights reserved.

Legal Notice: The content contained within this book may not be reproduced, duplicated, or transmitted without direct written permission from the author or the publisher.

Under no circumstances will any blame or legal responsibility be held against the publisher, or author, for any damages, reparation, or monetary loss due to the information contained within this book, either directly or indirectly.

This book is copyright protected. It is only for personal use. You cannot amend, distribute, sell, use, quote or paraphrase any part, or the content within this book, without the consent of the author or publisher.

ISBN: 978-1-7361555-2-3

Disclaimer: The universities and organizations mentioned in this book are used for illustrative and descriptive purposes only.

Their inclusion does not imply any affiliation with or endorsement by the institutions or organizations. All stories and characters are entirely fictional. Any resemblance to real people, places, or events is purely coincidental. The views and opinions expressed are those of the author and do not reflect those of any university or organization referenced.

TABLE OF CONTENTS

Introduction 7

Prologue: The Wisdom of the Train Keeper 9

Chapter 1: The Speaker at the Food Truck 13
Speaking with Clarity and Courage

Chapter 2: The Name Behind the Résumé 21
Personal Branding & Online Presence

Chapter 3: The Fear of Asking Questions 27
Learning to Ask Questions (Even When You're Afraid)

Chapter 4: The Silent Voice at the Roundtable 35
Speaking Up in Group Settings

Chapter 5: The Critique That Cut Deep 43
Receiving Feedback Gracefully

Chapter 6: The Clock That Nearly Cost Her the Job 51
Punctuality

Chapter 7: The Art of Speaking 59
Effective Communication

Chapter 8: The Power of the Right Allies 65
Collaboration & Choosing the Right Allies

Chapter 9: The Listener Who Opened Doors 73
Listening to Understand

Chapter 10: The Mountain She Chose to Climb 81
Growth Mindset

Chapter 11: The Weight of the Missed Email 87
Accountability

Chapter 12: The Pivot That Paid Off 95
Adaptability

Chapter 13: The Mirror Moment 101
Self-Awareness

Chapter 14: The Lesson in the Lobby 107
Professionalism

Chapter 15: The Day That Got Away 113
Time Management

Chapter 16: Taming the Spiral 121
Time Management (Creative, ADHD-Friendly)

Chapter 17: The Perspective That Changed Everything 129
Empathy

Chapter 18: The Line She Chose to Hold 137
Integrity

Chapter 19: The Connection at the Sign-In Table 145
Poise

Chapter 20: The Teammate Who Changed the Vibe 153
Positive Attitude

Chapter 21: The Contact They Almost Ignored 159
Proactive Problem Solving

Chapter 22: The Complaint She Didn't Make 165
Gratitude & Follow-Through

Chapter 23: The Jog That Opened a Door 171
Networking

Chapter 24: The Letters That Found Their Train 179
Passing It On

Personal Skills Assessment 186

Communication Skills 187

Monthly Progress Tracker 190

INTRODUCTION

One of the main reasons I wrote *From Invisible to Valuable* was because of an alarming headline I couldn't ignore: "Hiring managers would rather leave a job unfilled or give it to a robot than hire a new college graduate." In fact, many hiring managers believe that recent college graduates do not have the right skill sets.

That assertion is not science fiction. It's reality.

Too many smart, capable young people are entering the workforce without the essential skills that make someone not just hireable but valuable. Employers aren't just looking for degrees. They're looking for people who know how to communicate, think critically, show up on time, ask questions, and work well with others.

This book was created to help you do exactly that.

Whether you're a high school student preparing for your first job, a college or vocational student searching for an internship, or someone in the early stages of your career, *From Invisible to Valuable* is for you. This isn't focused on theory but real-world skills, the kind hiring managers actually care about.

Each chapter shares a fictional but relatable story set in a real-world location followed by three practical takeaways you can apply. These are the success skills no one teaches you, but everyone expects you to know.

If you want to land an internship or a job, make a great impression, and build a career that lasts, this book is your starting point.

I've taught thousands of young adults about financial education and essential skills, and I've had the privilege of guiding many of them as they take their first steps toward building successful careers. I've seen firsthand the transformation that happens when someone learns how to bring their best self forward.

Now it's your turn.

Let's get started,

Doron Noyman

Author | Mentor | Public Speaker

PROLOGUE: THE WISDOM OF THE TRAIN KEEPER

Dax was still holding the pen in his left hand as he gazed through the large window of his office on the 38th floor. He looked at the park, the street below, the cars, and the people rushing to get lunch.

It was the largest deal he had ever signed, 568 million dollars.

"Yes," he thought to himself, *"568 million dollars."*

From afar, he saw the train slowly rolling into the train station, and he smiled.

He closed his eyes and drifted into the past...

The station was alive with movement. The great iron beasts rumbled in and out, carrying men and women to distant places—some toward wealth, some toward adventure, and some toward unknown fates.

Among them stood Dax, a young man clutching a worn leather portfolio, his ticket to nowhere. He had been here before, watching others board their trains; their paths unfolding while he remained behind.

His resume was polished. His degree framed. His skills well-practiced. Yet, each time an opportunity approached, the doors remained closed.

He had studied late into the night. He had applied to dozens of jobs. He had followed the advice he had always been given—work hard, stay focused, and success will come.

Yet, it hadn't.

Frustration pressed against his ribs as another train pulled away, carrying a man no older than himself, a man who had once been his classmate.

"What did he do that I did not?" Dax murmured to himself.

"Ah, now that is the right question," came a voice.

Dax turned to see an old station keeper sitting on a nearby bench, adjusting his cap. His uniform was worn at the elbows, his beard streaked with gray, and his eyes carried the weight of many years of watching travelers come and go.

"You seem troubled, son," the keeper said.

Dax let out a long sigh. "I do not understand. I did all I was told. I worked hard. I built my skills. And yet, the world still does not see me. I knock, but no one answers."

The station keeper nodded, as if he had heard the story many times before. "Tell me, what is it you seek?"

Dax hesitated, then answered, "A chance. A door to open. To board the train to success."

The keeper chuckled, "And how do you expect to board if you do not know how to present your ticket?"

PROLOGUE: THE WISDOM OF THE TRAIN KEEPER

Dax frowned, "I have my credentials. My skills."

"And yet," the keeper said, "those alone do not open the door. Tell me, have you learned the art of speaking so others listen? Have you learned how to make yourself seen? Have you learned to read the signals of the world and step forward at the right moment?"

Dax shook his head. "I thought knowledge and hard work were enough."

"Ah," the keeper said, stroking his beard. "You are like many others before you. You believe that knowledge alone is the ticket. But the world does not work that way."

Dax sat beside the keeper, eager to hear more.

"There are many great lessons to boarding the train of success," the old man continued. "Like the art of speaking, for no man boards alone. The art of being seen, for no train stops for one who hides in the shadows. And the art of wisdom, for a traveler without direction is but a wanderer."

Dax leaned forward. "Teach me."

The keeper smiled gently, then turned his gaze to the platform.

"I could," he said. "But look around you. See those holding tickets in their hands? Each of them carries a lesson, a story that earned them a place on the train."

He looked back at Dax. "If you truly want to board, don't simply wait. Go. Ask them. Learn their stories."

"For each one," he added with a glint in his eye, "has something no one taught them, but everyone expected them to know."

CHAPTER 1: THE SPEAKER AT THE FOOD TRUCK

"The voice you unlock today may be the bridge someone else walks across tomorrow."

Late Night in Brooklyn

It was a Friday night in Brooklyn, the kind where the sidewalk buzzes with laughter, the trains rumble underground, and something in the air makes you believe anything could happen.

A small crowd had formed near a mid-sized food truck parked on a quiet side street in Bushwick. A hand-painted sign on the side read:

WORD.
Spoken Word + Loaded Fries.
Get Fed. Get Free.

The truck's side panel was rolled up like a curtain, revealing a mic, a speaker, and a fold-out stage bathed in yellow string lights. The scent of curry, cumin, and sriracha wafted through the air, mixing with roasted peanuts and hot oil. People milled around eating, chatting, and waiting for the next name to be called.

At the edge of the scene stood Jordan, a college freshman at NYU, still wearing her class hoodie and a secondhand pair of Doc Martens. A notebook bulged out of her crossbody bag. Her hands were stuffed in her pockets.

She hadn't meant to stay. She'd just come for fries.

Where Fear Lives

Jordan had been writing poems since middle school—quiet ones and angry ones, with lines about losing her dad, switching coasts and schools and names, and feeling like a blurry photograph in a room full of high-definition people.

But she'd never shared them. Not once.
Not online. Not out loud.
Not even with her best friend.

Back in high school, she'd once frozen during a class presentation, her face flushed, voice dry, and throat locked tight. Kids didn't even laugh. They just... looked away. That was worse.

After that, she made a rule: she'd let her writing speak for itself. And by that, she meant she'd keep it to herself.

Voices on the Street

The mic buzzed as someone stepped up. A girl in a velvet blazer spit fire about her grandmother's war stories. Someone else rapped about not fitting into the culture they were born into. Another read a letter they wrote but never sent.

Jordan stayed at the edge of the crowd, arms folded.

Something shifted when a tall guy took the mic and closed their set with the line: "Silence isn't peace, it's hiding in a hoodie with your truth zipped up."

CHAPTER 1: THE SPEAKER AT THE FOOD TRUCK

Jordan felt like they were talking directly to her.

Her hand brushed the folded paper in her hoodie pocket. It was a piece she'd written two weeks ago in the laundry room of her dorm: a poem about invisibility, shrinking to fit, and missing home and pretending otherwise.

A girl next to her nudged her gently. "You signing up?"

Jordan blinked. "I wasn't planning to."

The girl smiled. "Good. That means you probably should."

Unfolding the Paper

As the emcee announced "last call" Jordan found herself walking slow and uncertain toward the sign-up sheet taped to the truck's side panel.

She wrote her name with a sharpie that had almost run dry.

Her heart pounded louder than the music from the Bluetooth speaker.

When her name was called, she nearly turned to leave. But her feet moved forward instead.

She stepped up.

She pulled out the crumpled page.

Her hands shook. Her voice cracked on the first line. A few people looked up from their fries.

She kept reading.

Halfway through, she looked up. Someone was nodding. Another person snapped. One whispered "Bars" under their breath.

Jordan kept going. Louder now. Clearer.

She read the final line like it mattered: "Maybe disappearing was never the trick, maybe I was never meant to vanish in the first place."

There was no standing ovation.

There was something better.

There was stillness. There was knowing. There was respect.

After the Mic

Back near the condiments table, a guy with green hair tapped her shoulder.

"You're Jordan, right?"

She hesitated. "Yeah."

"I don't usually stay this long," he said. "But that last line? About not vanishing? That hit me."

Jordan blinked. "Thanks."

"No, really," he added. "I've been trying to write something about that exact thing for weeks. You just put it out there."

She didn't know what to say. So, she smiled.

She had spoken for herself.

But she had spoken for him, too.

And maybe for more.

Skill:
Speaking with Clarity and Courage

✅ You don't have to be perfect;
you just have to be honest.

✅ Speaking up isn't about the spotlight;
it's about connection.

✅ Your truth might be the words someone else needed the courage to say.

∼

Practice the Skill: Speaking with Clarity and Courage

🦴 1. Voice Note Truths

Record a 60-second voice memo answering one of these questions:

> What's something you wish more people knew about you?
>
> What's a moment you were proud of but didn't tell anyone?
>
> What's something you're afraid to admit but need to hear?

Why it works: Speaking aloud, even to yourself, helps train your voice to match your truth. You'll start to hear your voice as a tool, not an obstacle.

2. Open Mic, Closed Circle

Organize a "soft mic" session with two to three trusted friends. Everyone brings something—an idea, a short rant, or a journal entry—and gets 3 minutes to speak uninterrupted. No advice. Just listening.

Why it works: You learn to speak without editing yourself and practice being heard without performance.

3. Rehearse, Rewrite, Repeat

Pick something you care about—a cause, a belief, a personal story—and write a 1-minute pitch for it. Say it out loud. Then rewrite it using fewer buzzwords and more emotion. Say it again. What changed?

Why it works: Clarity grows from honesty. When you stop performing and start connecting, your voice becomes unforgettable.

CHAPTER 2: THE NAME BEHIND THE RÉSUMÉ

*"Your name arrives before you do.
Make sure it says something worth remembering."*

Edgewood Avenue, Atlanta

Marcus leaned over his laptop at a coffee bar in Atlanta's Old Fourth Ward, trying to keep his chai latte from sliding onto the pile of scribbled résumé drafts beside him.

It was his third time here this week. The café buzzed with creatives typing on cracked MacBooks, artists comparing portfolios, and a guy at the next table loudly pitching a collab project.

Outside, the street pulsed with vibrancy from murals and the sounds of scooters and the Marta train in the distance. Inside, Marcus stared at the open tab titled:

"Brightstar Agency–Summer Strategy Internship Application"

Across from him, Jade sipped cold brew, legs crossed and reviewing a deck she'd made for a nonprofit fashion pop-up.

"You're overthinking it," she said without looking up. "Just tell them what you told me. Branding is storytelling, and you know how to make people care."

Marcus nodded, but his stomach still twisted. "Yeah. But what if I'm just another voice in the scroll?"

The Past in Pixels

Brightstar Agency was big. Their campaigns were everywhere, from billboards in Midtown to micro-influencer series in Decatur. Landing an interview felt like a win already.

Marcus had the portfolio, a brand strategy minor, and two internships. He even had a side hustle helping small businesses design content that popped on TikTok.

But behind the credentials was something else.

Two years ago, in the middle of finals week and sleep-deprived scrolling, he'd tweeted:

"Why does @BrightstarAgency sound like a wellness MLM that sells candles made of dreams?"

He thought it was funny. Sarcastic. No harm meant.

He forgot it the next day.

The Interview That Turned

On the 17th floor of a glass office tower in Midtown, Marcus sat across from a woman with silver hoops and sharp eyes—Tanya Chen, Brightstar's creative director.

The interview had gone well. They'd laughed about Atlanta weather. She complimented his analysis of their latest TikTok campaign. Then, she clicked to the next slide.

It was a screenshot.

The tweet.

"That you?" she asked, her voice light but direct.

Marcus froze. "I… yeah. I guess I didn't think anyone would ever see that again."

Tanya closed her laptop slowly. "Well, here's the thing. We believe in evolution. People grow. But when you apply to shape how brands are perceived, your own voice matters online, too."

Marcus swallowed hard.

"Here's your opportunity," she said. "Tell me what you'd do next."

The Realization

Later, back on Edgewood, Marcus told Jade everything.

"She wasn't even mad or upset," he said. "But I knew I'd messed up."

"You didn't just tweet," Jade said gently. "You branded yourself without even realizing it."

He looked down at his phone. His bio still said "Marketing nerd. Likes snacks." His pinned tweet was a repost from a meme account. His Instagram was half inside jokes, half somewhat finished reels.

His résumé said strategy. But his feed said chaos.

The Rewrite

That night, Marcus made a list:

📝 Update bios with what he actually does: *Gen Z brand strategist. Content with a cause.*

📌 Pin a thread about a campaign he helped design for a local bookstore.

🗄️ Archive tweets that didn't align with the voice he wanted to carry.

📱 Switch his IG to a professional account, organize highlights, and add value-first captions.

🎙️ Create one short-form video walking through a simple brand mistake and how to fix it.

He didn't delete everything. He didn't become fake. He just became consistent.

One week later, Tanya messaged him on LinkedIn: "Impressed by how fast you adapted. If you're still interested, let's talk again, this time with our digital team."

He smiled. This time, his name said exactly who he was.

Skill: Personal Branding & Online Presence

✅ Your résumé is what you submit; your online presence is what gets remembered.

✅ Branding isn't about pretending; it's about showing up clearly and consistently.

✅ The internet doesn't forget, but it can evolve with you if you lead the story.

Practice the Skill:
Personal Branding & Online Presence

🌐 1. Audit Your Online Self

Google your name plus any usernames you use. Then visit your top 3 platforms (Instagram, TikTok, LinkedIn, etc.) and answer these questions:

> If someone saw this for the first time, what would they assume I care about?
>
> Does this align with the future I want?

Why it works: You can't manage your brand if you don't know what it already says.

✍️ 2. Write Your "About Me" Story

Craft a 3-sentence personal brand statement using this formula:

> I help [who you serve]
>
> do [what value you bring]
>
> by [how you uniquely show up]
> Example: *I help mission-driven brands connect with students by creating content that feels real, not forced.*

Why it works: Personal clarity becomes public confidence. When you know your story, others will, too.

🗒 3. Create One Intentional Post

Choose one platform and share something that reflects your voice and value. This could be:

> A short reel breaking down something you've learned.
>
> A tweet-thread on a project you're proud of.
>
> A carousel post explaining your creative process.

Why it works: Consistency builds reputation. One meaningful post can do more than a dozen generic ones.

CHAPTER 3: THE FEAR OF ASKING QUESTIONS

"If you're afraid to ask, you're choosing silence over success."

University of Michigan, Early November

It was cold. Not the kind of cold that bit, but the kind that made students pull their sleeves over their hands and tuck their chins into fleece.

Taryn ran toward the engineering building, her backpack thudding against her spine. Inside, her laptop was open to a half-finished lab report and a blinking message thread she'd been avoiding for days.

The wind tugged at her coat as she pulled open the doors to the Dow Building and joined the quiet parade of undergrads filing into the lecture hall.

She scanned the room. Same spots, same faces. Zeke, a sophomore with a curly ponytail and a NASA sticker on his laptop, was already typing. He seemed like the kind of guy who understood all this naturally.

Taryn, on the other hand, had memorized the schedule, copied every slide, rewatched the lectures twice... and still didn't understand how half the functions they were coding actually worked.

She took her seat near the middle. Not so close that she'd be called on. Not so far that she'd seem disengaged.

The Pattern of Quiet

She wanted to ask every time the professor paused and said, "Any questions before we move on?"

She looked at her notes. She had three questions. Always did.

But she shook her head. So did everyone else.

Because asking made you visible.

And visibility meant risk.

She remembered the last time she had raised her hand, back in high school during AP Physics. She'd asked something about torque, and a guy two rows over chuckled under his breath. The teacher paused, repeated the equation, and moved on. No one said anything, but she'd felt the heat in her face for hours.

Now, she told herself she'd figure it out later.

Except she wasn't figuring it out.

She was sinking. Quietly.

Discord Doesn't Judge (Until It Does)

The class message board was active. Taryn read it every night. People posted summaries, memes, and even vented about the homework load.

CHAPTER 3: THE FEAR OF ASKING QUESTIONS

Zeke was in there constantly, asking things like, "Does anyone else's code crash on input size 7?" or "Can we walk through slide 42 in office hours tomorrow?"

He asked freely, casually. And no one laughed. They helped. They thanked him.

She admired that but couldn't imagine herself doing the same.

Until Thursday night.

The Message That Shifted Everything

Taryn sat at a corner table in Sweetwaters Café, half-listening to the rain hit the window, laptop glowing. Her latest quiz grade sat on the screen: sixty-two percent.

Her stomach dropped.

Maybe she didn't belong in engineering after all.

She opened the message board. Read the scroll.

And then she saw it, Zeke again:

"I totally blanked on dynamic memory today. Anyone want to break it down together this weekend?"

Dozens of students had been in that class. But Zeke said what no one else would.

Her fingers hovered over the keyboard. For once, she didn't let the fear stop her.

"Hey. I've been super behind but too nervous to say anything. I'd really love to join."

Seconds later, the reply came.

"You're 100 percent not alone. Come through. Sunday, Pierpont basement."

Sunday: The Study Table

The basement study lounge smelled like dry-erase markers and leftover pizza. Taryn showed up five minutes early. Zeke waved her over. He was surrounded by laptops, cords, and half-eaten bagels.

Three others joined. And something amazing happened.

People asked questions. Dumb ones. Brilliant ones. Half-formed ones.

"Wait, why does malloc even need a pointer again?" "Can we just diagram the heap memory on paper?"

Taryn said almost nothing the first hour. But she listened. And then, slowly, she spoke up.

"So… is the reason it breaks because the memory address gets overwritten?"

Zeke blinked. "Yes! That's exactly it."

They kept going. By hour three, Taryn had drawn two diagrams on the whiteboard and suggested a fix for a code loop someone else had missed.

It didn't feel like exposure anymore.

It felt like collaboration.

The Lecture That Changed Everything

A week later, back in lecture hall, the professor paused and asked, "Any questions before we move on?"

CHAPTER 3: THE FEAR OF ASKING QUESTIONS

This time, Taryn raised her hand.

The professor smiled. "Yes?"

Her voice didn't shake.

"Can you walk through why the recursive call doesn't overwrite the base case?"

The professor nodded and launched into an example.

No one laughed. No one rolled their eyes.

When she looked around, two students were writing her question down.

The Career Fair

Months later, Taryn stood at the engineering career fair with her resume in hand at a booth for ClearEdge Solutions, a software firm known for mentoring early career talent.

The recruiter, a friendly woman in a teal hoodie, asked, "Any questions for me?"

Taryn nodded. "Yes, how do new hires typically ask for help on your team, and how is that encouraged?"

The recruiter's eyebrows lifted. "That's a fantastic question. Honestly, it tells me you're someone who knows how to grow."

A week later, the company emailed her for a second-round interview.

Skill:
Learning to Ask Questions
(Even When You're Afraid)

✅ Fear of looking foolish keeps people stuck. Growth begins when you ask.

✅ Most people are silently confused; asking out loud makes you a leader.

✅ Curiosity builds confidence. Start by asking, and you'll go further than those who pretend.

∼

Practice the Skill: Learning to Ask Questions (Even When You're Afraid)

1. Ask One Question On Purpos

In your next class, meeting, or Zoom call, make a deal with yourself: ask *one* thoughtful question. It doesn't have to be brilliant, just honest. Examples:

"Can you walk through that part again in a different way?"

"What would success look like for this project?"

Why it works: Practice builds confidence. One small ask trains your voice to show up.

2. Rewrite the "Dumb" Question

Think of a question you were too afraid to ask. Now write it down. Next, reframe it in two ways:

As a *clarifying* question

As a *collaborative* question

Examples:
- ✗ "I probably should know this, but I don't get it."
- ✓ "Can we break that part down again from the start?"
- ✓ "Can I walk you through my thinking and get your take?"

Why it works: How you ask changes how you're heard.

3. Question Journal Challenge (7 Days)

Keep a "Question Journal" for one week. Each day, write down:

One question you asked.

One question you wish you'd asked.

One thing that got clearer after asking.

Why it works: You'll start to notice patterns and prove to yourself that asking always leads to growth.

CHAPTER 4:
THE SILENT VOICE
AT THE ROUNDTABLE

*"A seat at the table means nothing
if you never learn to speak."*

Madison City Hall – Early Spring

The city was thawing. Slushy snow lined the edges of the sidewalks along Martin Luther King Jr. Boulevard, and puddles gleamed in the gutters near Madison's City-County Building. Eli stood at the bottom of the wide stone steps, glancing up at the entryway where he was expected to speak.

He'd never been inside city hall before.

He zipped up his thrifted puffer jacket and stepped into the lobby. A receptionist pointed him toward room 302 where the Youth Transit Roundtable was already gathering.

As he walked down the hallway, fluorescent lights buzzing above, he replayed the words his older sister had said that morning.

"You belong in that room, Eli. Don't let the ties and badges fool you."

Inside the Room

Room 302 smelled like coffee, whiteboard markers, and something faintly citrusy, probably the cleaning spray used that morning. It was lined with windows overlooking a still-icy Lake Monona. A horseshoe-shaped table sat in the middle, already half-occupied.

Eli clocked the details: printed name tags, water bottles from local nonprofits, clipboards stacked with color-coded data. The room was brighter and more formal than he'd imagined.

He found his name, written neatly on a folded card: Eli Reyes– La Follette High.

He sat near the edge.

To his left, Lucas, a junior from a charter school, was already talking about budget distribution and federal infrastructure funding. He sounded like a TED Talk.

To Eli, it felt like everyone else had taken debate class, internship prep, and some secret course in "How to Talk Like You Belong."

Why He Didn't Speak

Eli had lived in Madison his whole life. He worked part-time at Willow Leaf Market, a small grocery store on the East Side. His mom worked two jobs. His little brother caught the bus to middle school alone most mornings.

When buses were late, or didn't come, Eli biked to work. Through snow. Through wind. Once even through black ice.

But he didn't have the words for that, not the fancy, city-planning kind.

CHAPTER 4: THE SILENT VOICE AT THE ROUNDTABLE

He'd practiced what he might say. Rehearsed something about equity and access.

But now? Sitting at this table with city officials, interns from UW-Madison, and a few outspoken student delegates?

His throat tightened. He told himself:

"They already said that."
"They know more than I do."
"Don't mess this up."

The Nudge That Mattered

During a short break, Eli stood near the table of snacks, picking at the label on his water bottle.

A voice behind him said, "I've been watching you."

He turned. It was Ms. Ortega, a city transportation staffer with soft eyes and squeaky sneakers.

"I've seen you take more notes than anyone else," she said. "Your pen didn't stop moving."

He half-smiled. "Yeah, I just ... I think better when I write."

"You also haven't said a word yet," she said gently.

"I don't know if I have the right words."

Ortega looked at him, not unkindly.

"You don't need the perfect words. You just need your story. The numbers already have a voice. The people behind them don't."

Then she walked away.

The Moment Eli Found His Voice

Back at the table, a discussion had broken out about reducing late-night bus routes that had "consistently low ridership." Lucas cited a data set and argued that resources should be redirected to "routes with statistically significant youth traffic."

Eli felt his chest tighten. The bus they were talking about? That was his bus.

He stared at his notebook.

He could stay silent and go home. Or he could speak.

He raised his hand.

The room quieted. Someone nodded toward him.

His voice cracked slightly as he began.

"I don't have numbers. Just a story."

He cleared his throat.

"The bus you're talking about, that's how I get home from work. It's how my brother gets to tutoring on the South Side. I know it doesn't look like a lot of us ride it ... but maybe it's because we don't have another option. Or we're afraid it won't come at all."

He felt every eye on him.

"You can't count who's missing from the map. But I promise you we're there."

The silence stretched. Then someone from public works wrote something down.

Ms. Ortega gave him a nod. Lucas said nothing.

CHAPTER 4: THE SILENT VOICE AT THE ROUNDTABLE

After the Room Cleared

As Eli zipped up his coat, the youngest council member, a woman with a tablet tucked under her arm, stopped him.

"You changed how I think about that data. Thank you."

Eli looked out the window toward the thawing lake.

He hadn't just spoken. He'd been heard.

Skill:
Speaking Up in Group Settings

☑ Don't confuse someone else's confidence with credibility, your voice matters.

☑ Lived experience is a form of expertise. Speak from it.

☑ Sometimes the most powerful insight doesn't sound polished. It sounds honest.

∼

Practice the Skill: Speaking Up in Group Settings

1. "One Thought Per Meeting" Challenge

In your next group meeting, class, or event, set one goal. Contribute one idea, question, or reflection, even if it's brief. Prep it in advance if needed. Write it down. Practice saying it once to yourself.

Why it works: It builds the muscle of showing up vocally without waiting for perfection.

2. Reframe Your Inner Dialogue

Next time you feel the impulse to stay silent, pause and write down the thought stopping you (e.g., *"They already said that"*). Then reframe it like this:

"If I say it, it adds weight."

"My story might shift the room."

"They haven't heard it from me."

Why it works: It trains your brain to treat self-doubt like background noise, not a red light.

3. Draft Your "Lived Experience" Pitch

Write a two to three sentence version of a real-life experience that gives you perspective and credibility, even if it's not formal or professional. This is your reason for being in the room.

Example:

"I've worked weekends at a local café since I was sixteen. I've watched how changes in bus schedules impact who shows up late or doesn't show up at all. I'm not reading a case study; I'm living it."

Why it works: Your lived experience can open eyes, shift priorities, and make policy personal. You don't need credentials to

CHAPTER 5: THE CRITIQUE THAT CUT DEEP

"Feedback isn't failure, it's a mirror. Growth begins when you stop turning away."

Savannah College of Art and Design (SCAD) – Savannah, Georgia

Marley had always loved found materials. Ever since she was a kid painting on cereal boxes and gluing bottle caps to shoebox lids, she'd been drawn to things people threw away.

Now, at twenty, she stood in SCAD's Adler Hall, watching her final project–a suspended sculpture made of copper wire, recycled plexiglass, and LED strips–rotate gently under track lighting. It looked like a frozen cyclone. Intentional chaos. Her best work yet.

Her heart pounded, though not from excitement but dread.

The folding chairs in front of her weren't filled with friends, but with faculty: Professor Andy Rothman, head of 3D Media; Dr. Mike Sloane, visiting critic from New York; and Ben Evans, a local sculptor with a booming voice and sharp taste.

Marley's final review had begun.

The First Cuts

They let her speak first. She explained the concept. "It's a commentary on consumption and collapse, how our choices, layered and discarded, eventually tangle into something unsustainable."

She thought she had nailed it.

Then came the feedback.

"Visually compelling," Dr. Sloane began. "But crowded. Your material choices are strong, but I'm not sure what you're asking the viewer to feel."

"There's tension, yes," said Rothman, "but no pause. No moment of quiet in the chaos."

"Feels like you're still designing for approval, not clarity," added Evans. "What do you want us to walk away with? Guilt? Awe? Confusion?"

Marley froze, fingers clenching the hem of her flannel.

It wasn't just their words. It was their tone. Curious, calm, but not *impressed*.

She nodded. Said thank you.

But inside?

She burned.

CHAPTER 5: THE CRITIQUE THAT CUT DEEP

Why It Hurt So Much

Outside, the air was thick with early spring humidity. Spanish moss swayed lazily in the breeze as Marley walked aimlessly through the Historic District. Tourists laughed from pedicabs. A busker played acoustic guitar near Chippewa Square.

It all blurred.

She ended up at the café where art students gathered when they wanted to feel anonymous. She sat on the patio, barely touching her coffee.

This wasn't her first critique. But it was the first one that got past her armor.

Her piece mattered. Not because it was flashy, but because it came from her story. The wire was from broken bed frames she'd pulled from the alley behind her freshman dorm. The plexiglass came from her part-time job at a sign shop. This wasn't just a sculpture; it was her life.

And they didn't get it.

Or worse, they did, and still didn't think it was enough.

The Voice of Someone Who Understood

"Bad day?" asked Jules, sliding into the chair across from her.

Jules was two years older, a textile major with silver rings on every finger and a quiet confidence that made her seem unshakable. She'd taken Marley under her wing last year when Marley nearly dropped a class after a rough group project.

Marley didn't answer.

"Critique?" Jules guessed.

Marley nodded.

"They said it was too much. That I was hiding behind the idea. That it needed space. But this *is* me. This is how I see the world."

Jules took a sip of tea. "They're not attacking you, Mar. They're meeting you at your edge."

Marley blinked. "What does that even mean?"

"When you're just starting, people either hype you up or say nothing. But when they see you can go further, they push. They meet you at the edge of your current ability. And then invite you to step over it."

Marley looked away. "It still sucks."

"Of course it does. Feedback always stings. But the better you get, the sharper it becomes. That's how you know you're growing."

Back to Adler Hall

That night, Marley returned to the studio alone. The room smelled like glue, sawdust, and stress.

Her sculpture looked different now. Not ruined. But exposed.

She circled it, sketchbook in hand, writing down what each section was doing. Which parts worked. Which didn't. Which moments were loud, and which had no air.

She didn't trash it. She refined it.

She removed three chaotic wire loops, opened space in the core, and dimmed the LED strips so the light felt like breath instead of static.

She didn't try to please her critics.

She tried to speak *clearly*.

Two Weeks Later – Gallery Night

The student gallery was packed. Her revised piece now hung in a corner alcove, softly lit. It breathed. It held tension and silence. It asked for attention without shouting for it.

Professor Rothman stopped in front of it, arms crossed.

"You found the pause," she said.

Marley nodded. "Still figuring out the language."

"That's all any of us are doing."

Dr. Sloane took a photo. Ben Evans gave her a quiet nod.

Jules, across the room, raised her glass.

Skill: Taking Feedback Without Falling Apart

✅ Feedback isn't rejection; it's refinement.

✅ If it didn't matter, they wouldn't offer critique. Listening is a sign of maturity.

✅ You don't grow by defending your work. You grow by re-seeing it.

∼

✍️ Practice the Skill:
Taking Feedback Without Falling Apart

⊞ 1. "Cool Down Before You Rewrite" Ritual

Next time you get critique, on schoolwork, a project, or even a post, don't respond right away. Set a 20-minute timer. Walk. Vent in your Notes app. Breathe. Then return and ask: "What part of this feedback stings because it's true?"

Why it works: It helps separate emotion from insight so you can respond instead of react.

✏️ 2. Create a "Critique Decoder" List

Write down common phrases you've heard in feedback and translate them into actionable takeaways.

Example:

> "Feels a little crowded" → Try removing one to two elements.
>
> "What are you trying to say?" → Clarify your core message in one sentence.
>
> "Could use more depth" → Add one layer of personal story or context.

Why it works: It turns vague critique into concrete edits and builds your revision toolkit.

🎨 3. Reframe the Critique (Practice Statement)

Write a two to three sentence response to remind yourself feedback isn't a verdict. It's a mirror.

Example:

"It's hard to hear this because I care. But if someone took time to respond, that means my work got their attention. Now I get to make it clearer, stronger, and more honest."

Why it works: It puts you back in creative control, without shutting down your growth.

CHAPTER 6: THE CLOCK THAT NEARLY COST HER THE JOB

"Being late isn't about time. It's about trust."

Lakewood, Colorado – The Offer That Changed Everything

Nia Brooks had always been the type to juggle too much. She was in her second year at Red Rocks Community College, majoring in digital media, working part-time at a local café, and running a tiny freelance business designing social posts for local yoga studios. Her calendar was a color-coded collage of class times, project deadlines, and reminders to eat.

When she got the internship offer from NorthStar, a boutique creative agency in Denver's LoDo district, she cried. It was the kind of place that didn't usually look twice at community college students.

"We loved your reel," the creative director had said during her Zoom interview. "You have real storytelling instincts."

It was her shot. Her chance to step inside the world she dreamed of.

The welcome email was clear:

"Start Monday. 9 a.m. sharp."

A Rocky Start

That first Monday, she meant to be early.

After closing the café the night before, she didn't get home until 12:45 a.m. She fell asleep on the couch, missed her first alarm, frantically sprang awake, ran to the train, and waited for the light rail on a platform slick with spring slush.

She arrived at NorthStar at 9:14 a.m. sweaty, apologetic, and out of breath.

Tasha, the associate creative director, raised her eyebrows. "Morning, Nia. Glad you made it."

Nia forced a smile. "Sorry, the train was late."

Tasha nodded once. "Let's get you set up."

When a Pattern Becomes a Problem

It didn't stop there.

A week later, Nia walked in at 9:08, breathless from running three blocks. Then 9:11. Then 9:19. There was always a reason.

Train delays.
Alarm failure.
Rain.
A spilled coffee.
A late café shift the night before.

But even when she smiled and apologized, she noticed the shift in tone. The tighter "good mornings." The way they stopped assigning her to client call prep and instead handed her admin overflow.

CHAPTER 6: THE CLOCK THAT NEARLY COST HER THE JOB

One Thursday, she walked into a strategy huddle five minutes late and found someone else in her seat.

She laughed it off. But inside, something twisted.

The Talk

On a gray, drizzly Tuesday, Tasha stopped by Nia's desk after a team check-in.

"Can I steal five minutes?"

They walked to a side conference room with glass walls and pastel sticky notes everywhere.

Nia sat. So did Tasha. She folded her hands gently.

"You're talented, Nia. That's not in question."

Nia's chest tightened as she registered the tone, supportive but edged.

"But," Tasha continued, "punctuality is a reflection of reliability. And when you're not here on time, it affects more than your own day. It throws off meetings. Hand-offs. Team rhythm. People hesitate to depend on someone who might not be there when they're needed."

Nia opened her mouth, then closed it.

"We want to invest in you," Tasha said, softer now. "But we need to see that you take this opportunity seriously enough to show up for it every single day."

The Impact Hit Later

That night, Nia sat in her studio apartment in Lakewood with the lights off, the town glowing faintly through the blinds.

She pulled up her home screen. Her lock screen said: "You were chosen. Act like it."

She hadn't been late because she didn't care. She was just overwhelmed. Overcommitted. Always behind.

But now, her dream job was on the line, and she realized it didn't matter how talented she was if people couldn't count on her to show up.

She set her alarms. Three of them. She rerouted her commute. She moved her café shift to evenings only. She built a spreadsheet called "Time Is Trust." And she wrote on her mirror: Early is a gift. On time is respect.

What Changed

The next day, she was at NorthStar at 8:43. Then 8:39. By the next week, she was already at her desk when Tasha arrived.

She started keeping a list of daily deliverables. She prepped her files the night before. She offered to open team meetings. She stopped apologizing and started being present.

One morning, the creative director passed her in the break room.

"Hey, you're the first one here every day now."

She smiled. "Trying to make time my ally."

He laughed. "You're already someone we rely on."

Skill:
Punctuality

✅ Being on time is a small habit with big consequences.

✅ People don't just remember your work. They remember your presence.

✅ Punctuality earns trust, and trust opens doors.

∼

Practice the Skill: Punctuality

1. Build a "Backwards Buffer"

Pick one regular commitment this week (class, work, gym, etc.). Instead of planning to arrive "on time," plan to arrive fifteen minutes early.

Work backward. How long does the commute take? What time do you have to leave? What time do you need to start getting ready?

Why it works: It shifts you from reactive to proactive time management and removes last-minute chaos from your day.

2. Set Your "Time Anchors"

Choose two key events in your week and anchor them with a digital habit:

> Set a recurring calendar alert 1 hour before.
>
> Create a custom lock screen with your mantra
> (e.g. Early is a gift. On time is respect.)
>
> Use a music playlist that lasts the exact length of your commute as your cue.

Why it works: It turns being on time into a rhythm, not a panic.

🧠 3. Track the Trust

For one week, keep a short journal log:

> What time did you arrive?
>
> How did it feel?
>
> Did being early or on time change how people interacted with you?
>
> Did it change how you felt about yourself?

Why it works: It links the emotional and social impact of punctuality to your daily actions, so it's not just about time, it's about trust.

CHAPTER 7:
THE ART OF SPEAKING

"A person who speaks to be heard makes noise; a person who speaks to be understood makes progress."

Palo Alto, California – Heart of Silicon Valley

The soft clack of keyboards filled the coworking space just off University Avenue. Outside, electric scooters zipped by sunlit cafés where engineers talked code over cold brews. Inside, Alex sat hunched over his laptop, tweaking slide animations no one ever seemed to notice.

He wasn't new to this world. A self-taught developer since high school, Alex attends a local community college and also works on his startup. He'd built a productivity app that could save businesses hours of manual work. Everyone said it was brilliant.

But brilliant hadn't closed any deals.

After his fourth pitch in three weeks ended with another "We'll think about it," Alex found himself nursing a lukewarm coffee at his usual café, Taproot. He stared at his inbox. It was empty, and so was he.

"I don't get it," he muttered. "I explain all the features. I show them the demo. Why don't they see it?"

A voice from the next table replied without invitation. "You sound like a guy selling a compass to people who just want to get home."

Alex turned. A man with a salt-and-pepper beard and a cardigan over a faded startup hoodie smiled and extended a hand.

"Samuel. You pitched next to me on Tuesday. Good stuff, just not sticking the landing."

Alex raised an eyebrow. "What do you mean?"

Samuel pulled out a notebook. "You're pitching features. But clients don't buy features. They buy relief."

He flipped the notebook to a blank page and drew a simple curve. "See this? It's not about the tool. It's about the tension."

Alex frowned. "But I built the tool to fix the tension."

Samuel leaned in. "Then talk about *that*. Imagine someone's drowning. You're explaining the buoyancy of the rope when they just need you to throw it."

Rewriting the Pitch

Over the next hour, they sat at the sun-drenched window table surrounded by startup posters and overheard investor gossip. Samuel played role after role–restaurant owner, freelance consultant, overwhelmed office manager–while Alex practiced.

"Start with a question," Samuel coached. "A real one they feel in their gut."

By the time they finished, Alex had revised his pitch from a list of features into a conversation starter:

"How much time do you spend redoing reports because of tiny errors? What if you could get that time back and have confidence in the numbers?"

The First Real Connection

A week later, Alex was at a local tech networking mixer near Stanford. He spotted a restaurant tech consultant near the bar and struck up a casual conversation.

Instead of opening with a description of his software, he asked: "What's the part of your day that eats up the most time and gives the least reward?"

The man laughed. "Ugh, inventory reports. They're always wrong, and my name's on them."

Alex smiled. "That's exactly what I've been working on fixing."

They grabbed a table. Alex shared a simple before-and-after graphic on his phone. For once, no jargon. Just empathy, clarity, and a clear result.

By the end of the conversation, Alex had his first paying client.

What Came After

A few months later, Alex and Samuel met again in the same café, though there was a decidedly different vibe.

"How's it going?" Samuel asked.

"Turns out when I stop trying to sound smart and just try to be helpful, people say yes more."

Samuel raised his cup. "Now you're speaking their language."

Skill:
Speaking with Clarity and Impact

☑ Speak to solve, not to impress. Lead with the problem you solve, not the tool you built.

☑ People tune out jargon. Use plain language, stories, or metaphors to get your point across.

☑ Communication isn't a performance; it's a bridge. Meet people where they are.

∼

Practice the Skill: Speaking with Clarity and Impact

1. Start with the Pain, Not the Product

Pick something you're working on—a group project, a business idea, or a class presentation.

Now answer: *What real-life frustration does this solve?*

Rewrite your intro or pitch to start there.

Why it works: People don't connect to tools; they connect to problems they recognize.

2. Use the "Rope" Test

Explain your project or idea to someone outside your field (a sibling, your barista, a friend in a different major).

Don't use any jargon. Don't list features.

Instead, use a metaphor or simple scenario that shows why it matters.

Why it works: If they get it and care about it, you're speaking clearly. If they don't, refine until they do.

📄 3. Record a 60-Second "Problem > Transformation > Solution" Video

Structure your video like this:

1. A relatable problem
2. The change you want to create
3. How your idea makes it possible

Then watch it back. Ask yourself: *Would I care if I didn't already know this?*

Why it works: Video forces clarity. You'll catch filler, confusion, or over-explaining, and start communicating like someone worth listening to.

CHAPTER 8: THE POWER OF THE RIGHT ALLIES

"A lone builder tires before the wall is raised, but those who build together reach greater heights."

Old North St. Louis – A Business Plan, a Deadline, and Too Many Opinions

Camille Harper didn't play well with teams. She wasn't rude or arrogant. Just efficient. Precise. In her business classes at WashU, she was always the one rewriting the group deck at midnight and fixing the numbers before the presentation.

To her, "teamwork" often meant doing everything and pretending it was a group effort.

When she earned a spot in the Future of the City Fellowship, a summer program focused on community entrepreneurship and urban revitalization, she was proud.

Until she learned she'd be working on a team project.

A real one. With real people. And no professor to override them.

Four Visions, One Venture

The challenge: design and launch a pop-up business or initiative that brought value to the Old North neighborhood of St. Louis and reflected the community's story.

Their shared workspace sat above a coffee shop on 14th Street, where the hum of espresso machines underscored every brainstorming session.

Her team included:

> Riley, a social media strategist who believed in bold, disruptive campaigns and thought every idea needed a viral hook.
>
> Tomas, a nonprofit studies major who wanted to focus on storytelling and deep community listening.
>
> Aisha, an urban planning student passionate about cooperative business models and cultural sustainability.

Camille had a vision: a streamlined pop-up market, clean branding, and minimal overhead. It could be up and running in a month.

She presented her slide deck on day two.

Riley raised an eyebrow. "Looks like a startup pitch for a venture capitalist."

"Exactly," Camille said. "It's scalable."

Aisha tilted her head. "But is it meaningful? Where's the cultural connection? The soul?"

Tomas looked around the room. "Whose story is this telling, ours or the neighborhood's?"

Camille stiffened. "We're trying to make something *work*. That's the story."

Chapter 8: The Power of the Right Allies

Trying to Go It Alone

That night, Camille stayed up revising her plan.

She built a complete financial model. Logistics. Sourcing. A polished slide deck.

She brought it to the next meeting. But the room stayed quiet.

"It's a solid business," Riley said finally. "But it's not a *collaboration*."

Tomas added, "It doesn't leave space for anyone else's voice."

Camille packed up her laptop early and left the meeting in silence.

A Porch Conversation

Later that evening, she walked past the future site for the pop-up. The lot sat next to an old brick building that once housed a bakery, now boarded up.

Across the street, a woman in a flowered headscarf swept her front steps.

"You one of the students working on that project?" she called out.

Camille nodded. "We're launching a market here. Or... trying to."

The woman smiled. "That lot's seen a lot. Markets, music, and performance art events. We used to set up booths during Juneteenth and sell everything from pie to poetry."

Camille blinked. "Really?"

"Oh, yes. But it only worked when folks worked together. One person can build a booth. But it takes a block to build something that lasts."

She gently tapped her broom handle against the sidewalk.

"Just don't forget who you're building it for."

The Shift

At the next meeting, Camille didn't bring a presentation.

She brought iced coffee. And blank paper.

"Okay," she said. "What do *you* think this community actually needs? Let's build it together."

They talked. Sketched. Debated.

Riley proposed a community storytelling booth tied to a photo series. Aisha suggested collaborating with local artisans. Tomas reached out to neighborhood elders about setting up poetry readings and oral histories.

Camille still ran point on budgeting and logistics, but this time, she made space.

To her surprise, the idea grew richer. More real.

What They Built

They called it The Corner Collective, a weekend pop-up that celebrated local makers, storytellers, and entrepreneurs. One tent sold handmade soaps. Another hosted a live podcast recording with local activists. Camille set up a digital tip jar and QR codes for donations.

Over the weekend, over 500 people stopped by.

Even the woman from the porch came and brought sweet rolls to sell.

What Came After

CHAPTER 8: THE POWER OF THE RIGHT ALLIES

A week later, Camille sat on the bus back to campus.

She opened her email to find a note from one of the local vendors:

> "You didn't just help me sell candles. You helped me tell my story. Thank you for building something real."

Camille smiled and typed back:

> "It wasn't just me. It was a group effort, and I have the best partners."

Skill: Collaboration & Choosing the Right Allies

☑ You don't have to do everything alone and shouldn't.

☑ The best ideas don't come from control. They come from contribution.

☑ Real leadership means making room at the table, not building the table alone.

∼

Practice the Skill: Collaboration & Choosing the Right Allies

1. Map Your Collaboration Gaps

Think about a project, goal, or creative idea you're working on. Now write down three things:

    What you do best
    What you don't enjoy or struggle with
    Who you need beside you (specific strengths, not names)

Why it works: It helps you move from "I have to do it all" to "Who complements my skills?"

2. Run a "Build It Together" Session

In your next group project or meeting, resist showing a finished plan. Instead, come with a sketch or outline and ask:

    "What's missing?"
    "Where do you see yourself in this?"
    "What could make this more meaningful?"

Why it works: People support what they help shape. Collaboration grows when everyone sees their fingerprint on the outcome.

❈ 3. Create a Personal "Ally Filter"

Write out your values, what matters to you in work and relationships. Then list three traits or habits you look for in collaborators (e.g., reliability, creativity, compassion). Use this filter before saying yes to team projects or partnerships.

Why it works: You stop choosing people based only on availability or popularity and start choosing based on alignment.

CHAPTER 9: THE LISTENER WHO OPENED DOORS

"People remember how well you listened long after they forget what you said."

Philadelphia, PA – The Networking Room with No Air

Mira stood near the back wall of the student ballroom at Temple University, gripping a sweating cup of lemonade and trying not to overthink every movement. The air buzzed with the hum of introductions, business card swaps, and rehearsed elevator pitches. It was the university's spring networking mixer for communications majors, and one name towered above all the others on the invite list:

Solenne Navarro, Director of Strategic Communications at Purpose & More, a mission-driven agency known for launching bold campaigns with social impact across Philadelphia.

Everyone wanted a shot at the coveted summer internship Solenne was offering. It was paid, came with mentorship, and practically guaranteed post-grad job offers. Mira wanted it too, but not badly enough to elbow her way into a circle and rattle off her credentials like a radio jingle.

Instead, she listened to students exaggerate their projects, noticing how Solenne smiled politely but seemed to be scanning for the exit. She felt the subtle tension that always filled rooms where everyone wanted something, and few stopped to ask why.

The Moment She Didn't Plan

Later, Mira spotted Solenne near the food table, fumbling with a cocktail napkin and a full plate of plantain sliders.

"Need a hand?" Mira asked.

Solenne laughed, grateful. "Yes, please. I should've brought a tray."

Mira held the plate while Solenne grabbed a soda. The two stepped away from the crowd, settling near the windows overlooking Broad Street.

"I'm Mira," she offered. "Strategic comms major. And you look like you've been answering a lot of the same questions tonight."

Solenne grinned. "You noticed?"

"I guess I'm more of a listener than a talker," Mira said.

"Honestly? That's refreshing."

Instead of launching into a pitch, Mira asked, "What's been the most unexpectedly difficult part of growing a values-based brand in Philly?"

Solenne blinked then exhaled.

"You know, no one's asked me *that* tonight."

CHAPTER 9: THE LISTENER WHO OPENED DOORS

She leaned in and shared about balancing client demands with authenticity and fighting performative allyship while still trying to do good and make payroll. Mira asked thoughtful follow-ups and let Solenne finish her thoughts. She nodded, responding with

curiosity instead of solutions. She caught the pauses others might rush past.

They talked for nearly twenty minutes.

The Wait Afterward

The next morning, Mira drafted a thank-you email but hesitated before sending it.

"Did I say enough?" she wondered. "Did I sound interested? Or just awkward?"

Compared to others at the event, she hadn't listed her experience or asked for the internship. She had asked questions. Listened. Left it there.

She hit send.

And waited.

The Subject Line That Changed Everything

Five days later, the subject line hit her inbox:

Let's Talk Summer

Solenne's note was short:

"I don't need someone who can talk the loudest. I need someone who listens deeply, because that's who clients trust. You in?"

Mira grinned.

The Internship That Spoke Volumes

By July, Mira was sitting in brainstorming meetings at Purpose & More's office. The walls were lined with sticky notes and campaign wireframes. While others jumped in to pitch taglines or content hooks, Mira observed, jotted notes, and spoke when she had something others had missed.

In one meeting, a client from a local housing nonprofit expressed frustration.

"We're tired of campaigns that look polished but don't reflect our actual community."

The room tensed. Someone started to respond defensively, but Mira gently interrupted.

"Can I ask, what does 'reflect' mean to you?"

That pause changed the entire meeting. The client opened up. Mira asked three more questions that no one else had thought to ask.

Later that afternoon, Solenne stopped by her desk.

"That's what I meant," she said. "Most people talk to be clever. You listen to understand. That's rare."

What Came After

Mira didn't become the loudest voice in the room.

She became the one people turned to when they actually wanted to be heard.

Skill:
Listening to Understand
(Not Just to Respond)

☑ Listening is more than silence; it's curiosity in action.

☑ Asking the right questions shows more confidence than filling space.

☑ People remember how you made them feel heard more than how you made them feel impressed.

∼

Practice the Skill: Listening to Understand (Not Just to Respond)

1. The 70/30 Rule Experiment

In your next conversation, whether it's with a friend, professor, or classmate, aim to speak thirty percent of the time and listen seventy percent. Ask one follow-up question for every statement you make. Try not to interrupt or finish their sentences.

Why it works: It rewires your instinct to respond quickly and teaches you to *stay with* someone else's thoughts longer.

2. The "Reflect + Clarify" Drill

Next time you're in a conversation, try this simple pattern:

> Step 1: Reflect what they said
> ("It sounds like you felt overlooked in that meeting.")
>
> Step 2: Clarify their meaning
> ("What part bothered you most?")

Why it works: It shows people you're not just hearing them; you're making space for their full experience.

🎯 3. Design Your "Listening Reputation"

Ask yourself: *How do I want people to describe me after we talk?*

Write three adjectives you want associated with your communication style (e.g., present, curious, calm).

Then write two behaviors you'll start doing to live those out (e.g., put your phone away, pause before responding).

Why it works: Being intentional about how you want to be known helps you build trust that lasts longer than any first impression.

CHAPTER 10: THE MOUNTAIN SHE CHOSE TO CLIMB

"Some mountains are made of rock. Others are made of self-doubt. Either way, step by step is how you rise."

Flagstaff, Arizona – Northern Arizona University

Karina stared out at Mount Elden; its outline clear against the deep-red Arizona sky. She was supposed to be reviewing data models for her environmental science class, but her brain had shut down three graphs ago. The problem wasn't the graphs. The problem was what they were beginning to represent.

Failure.

Karina had always been good at school. Not exceptional but solid. She'd chosen environmental science because she loved it and grew up hiking, collecting leaves, and scribbling plant names into the margins of her notebooks. But college was different. Data & Modeling 202 was where it all fell apart.

Two failed quizzes. A lab partner who stopped texting her back. A professor who circled half her project in red. And the worst part? She couldn't shake the thought:
Maybe I'm not built for this.

The Hike Starts Ugly

Karina didn't talk much in class. But Bea, a senior TA with a messy bun and trail-worn Chacos, noticed her slumped posture in the back row.

"Want to study together sometime?" Bea asked one afternoon. "I used to get wrecked by this class, too."

Karina blinked. "Really? You seem like you live and breathe Excel."

Bea laughed. "Only after failing my first stats midterm."

They met at a local café later that week. Bea explained concepts with metaphors, data points as hikers, and models as weather patterns. For the first time, Karina didn't feel dumb. Just… new.

"You don't have to sprint up the mountain," Bea said, sipping her coffee. "You just have to keep moving."

Step by Step

Karina started climbing.

She made a spreadsheet to track how often she asked questions in class, one tick per hand raise.

She rewrote her notes into "teach-back" summaries, pretending she had to explain them to a friend.

She watched YouTube tutorials late at night instead of doom-scrolling.

She emailed her professor weekly with one specific, focused question.

The progress wasn't dramatic, but it was steady.

The D+ became a C. The C became a B-. Suddenly, she wasn't gasping for air at the base of the mountain.

The Trail Turns

During a group project analyzing local water use, Karina's team hit a roadblock. Their regression model wasn't matching the real-world patterns.

"What if the issue is seasonality?" Karina offered. "Like, irrigation spikes in summer. Maybe that's skewing the trend line?"

Everyone paused. Someone double-checked the data. She was right.

Her voice didn't shake. Her teammates didn't look surprised.

They just listened.

The Summit Isn't the End

By finals week, Karina had climbed higher than she'd thought possible. She still had questions. Still needed help sometimes. But now she *expected* to improve.

She wasn't "bad at data." She was still getting better.

And when she passed Mount Elden on her walk home, she finally looked up and thought:

I don't have to conquer it today. I just have to keep going.

Skill: Growth Mindset

☑ Struggle means you're trying, not that you're failing.

☑ Intelligence isn't fixed. It grows with effort, feedback, and patience.

☑ The question isn't "Am I good at this?" It's "What can I learn next?"

~

Practice the Skill: Growth Mindset

1. Rewrite the Failure Script

Pick one recent "failure", a bad grade, a botched interview, a missed opportunity.

Now rewrite the narrative using this formula:

"I didn't [result], but I learned [lesson], and I'm now trying [new approach]."

Example:
"I didn't get the internship, but I learned I need clearer examples in interviews. I'm now preparing a story bank to practice with a friend."

Why it works: It reframes failure as fuel instead of a final stop.

2. Track "Tiny Wins"

Create a simple 7-day log in your Notes app or journal. Each day, list one small win, something you understood, improved, or kept showing up for.

Even if it's "Didn't give up."

Example:
- ✓ Watched a tutorial even though I didn't feel like it
- ✓ Asked one clarifying question in class
- ✓ Rewrote confusing notes in my own words

Why it works: It trains your brain to notice *progress* instead of just perfection.

🔄 3. Swap "I Can't" with "I'm Learning To"

Each time you catch yourself saying "I can't ___," pause and reframe it as:

"I'm learning to ___, and that takes time."

Examples:

"I can't code" → "I'm learning to think like a coder, and that takes time."

"I can't do public speaking" → "I'm learning to speak with confidence, even if I shake."

Why it works: Language shapes mindset. This small shift builds self-compassion and momentum.

CHAPTER 11: THE WEIGHT OF THE MISSED EMAIL

"Credibility isn't built on perfection. It's built on what you do when you drop the ball."

Downtown Los Angeles – A Campaign, a Deadline, and a Choice

Zaria adjusted the fan on her desk for the third time. Even in late September, the heat in their downtown LA office refused to quit. The walls of the old, converted warehouse pulsed with the hum of startup energy. Open seating, Slack notifications, and cold brew on tap abounded.

She was six weeks into her internship at CleanWater, a mission-driven organization focused on water justice in California. Their latest campaign? A bilingual outreach push across East Valley neighborhoods affected by recurring water shutoffs.

Zaria was proud to be part of it. She'd grown up in a Fresno neighborhood where boil-water notices were routine. This work wasn't abstract; it was personal.

So when Ellie, her supervisor, asked her to confirm final logistics with the campaign's coalition partners and send the official rollout email by Friday, Zaria had said, "Absolutely."

She meant it.

The Mistake

On Monday morning, Zaria was halfway through checking edits on a social media caption when she saw the message from Ellie:

"Hi, any reason the East Valley rollout didn't go out Friday? Just heard from the partners. They never got it."

Her stomach dropped.

She clicked into her "Drafts" folder.

There it was. The email she had written and reviewed ... but never sent.

Zaria's face flushed. Her throat tightened. She imagined the ripple effect—missed press, confused volunteers, wasted prep hours.

She hovered over the reply button.

Do I say the email didn't send? That I thought I hit send? That something must've glitched?

No. She knew what had happened.

She'd gotten overwhelmed. She'd over-prioritized social media metrics. And she had forgotten.

CHAPTER 11: THE WEIGHT OF THE MISSED EMAIL

Plain and simple.

The Decision

She stood up and walked past the standing desks and whiteboards filled with color-coded strategy timelines.

In the restroom mirror, she saw the anxiety in her eyes.

She took a breath.

Then she opened Slack and typed.

"Hey Ellie, this one's on me. I wrote the email but forgot to send it. I didn't double-check Friday, and I apologize. I'm resending now and will personally call each coalition lead to confirm delivery. If there's anything I can do to repair the delay, I'm on it."

She hit send.

Then she sat back and waited.

What Accountability Sounds Like

A few minutes later, Ellie replied.

"Thanks for owning it. Everyone drops something eventually. What matters is how you show up after. Let me know how the calls go."

Zaria let out a breath she hadn't realized she was holding.

She picked up the phone. Called each partner. Took notes on what they needed. Apologized without making excuses.

By that evening, the campaign was back on track, and she was exhausted.

But she didn't feel crushed.

She felt *clear*.

What Came After

Later that week, Ellie dropped by her desk.

"Zaria," she said, "you took a hit and handled it like a pro. The truth is mistakes don't break trust, denial does."

Zaria nodded. "I never want to be the person who blames the software."

Ellie smiled. "You won't be. You're already the person who takes responsibility and keeps moving."

What She Built

Zaria went home that night and built her own tool. It was nothing fancy, just a personal dashboard that tracked major deadlines, sent her daily reminders, and pinged her if anything sat in Drafts for more than twenty-four hours.

She called it her *Check Yourself* tab.

It didn't make her perfect.

It made her aware.

And that was enough.

Skill: Accountability

✅ People don't expect you to be flawless. They expect you to be honest.

✅ Accountability isn't about blame; it's about ownership and repair.

✅ Mistakes will happen. How you respond is what defines your reputation.

∼

Practice the Skill: Accountability

1. Start an "Accountability Mirror" Log

Each night, jot down:

- 1 thing you said you'd do
- Whether or not you did it
- What you'll do differently tomorrow

Keep it honest, short, and judgment-free. This isn't punishment; it's personal data.

Why it works: It builds awareness of your follow-through and helps you close the gap between intention and action.

2. Send the "Own It" Text or Email

Next time you miss a deadline, forget something, or mess up, don't explain it away.

Try this formula:

- Own the action ("I missed the deadline.")
- Acknowledge the impact ("I know that added pressure to the team.")
- Share your next step ("I've blocked time to finish it, and it will be done by 2 p.m.")

Why it works: This simple framework builds trust fast, especially with professors, supervisors, or collaborators.

🧠 3. Audit Your "Excuse Patterns"

Make a list of your most common excuses (e.g., "I was too busy," "I didn't know," "My alarm didn't go off").

Next to each, write a tiny shift you could make:

"Too busy" → Prioritize or say no sooner.

"Didn't know" → Ask or clarify up front.

"Alarm" → Set two and place your phone across the room.

Why it works: You can't change what you won't name. This helps you spot habits that chip away at your credibility and fix them before they become patterns.

CHAPTER 12:
THE PIVOT THAT PAID OFF

"Flexibility isn't failure. It's intelligence in motion."

San Jose, California – Innovation Jam, Day One

The whiteboard walls were already scribbled with big ideas. Ava Cruz walked into the coworking hub in downtown San Jose and could feel the caffeine, ambition, and startup energy in the air. Laptops hummed. Teams clustered around sketches and slide decks. LED wristbands blinked, marking who was checked in.

She adjusted her lanyard. SolveLab 36: Silicon Valley Edition. 36 Hours. Solve a Real Problem. Pitch. Win.

Ava was a junior studying data science at San José State. She'd applied on a whim after hearing the word "social impact" buried in the application materials.

Now she was here, with a team she'd met an hour ago:

    Niko, a machine learning whiz with swagger and speed.

    Lexi, a visual designer obsessed with motion graphics.

Raj, a front-end developer who spoke mostly in code snippets.

They brainstormed fast and settled on an idea quickly: a smart parking app that used predictive analytics to help drivers find free street spots near downtown.

It looked good on the whiteboard. It ticked the "innovation" box. But something inside Ava itched.

The Question No One Asked

They were twenty minutes into wireframing when Ava paused. "Can I ask something?"

Niko was sketching icons.

"Who are we developing this for?" she asked. "Because I'm thinking about my grandma in East San Jose. She doesn't own a car. She walks to the library for Wi-Fi. Who's building for her?"

Niko frowned. "This is a tech jam. We're solving for efficiency. Traffic. Real-world pain points."

"But only for people already inside the system," Ava said. "What about the ones tech usually leaves out?"

Lexi looked up. "What are you thinking?"

Ava took a breath. "What if instead of a parking app, we built something that helps people, like my grandma, access tech training, library Wi-Fi, digital services? A tool to bridge the divide. Not widen it."

Raj hesitated. "We'd have to scrap the whole code base."

"We'd be starting over," Niko added.

Ava nodded. "We would. But maybe we'd actually help someone."

The Pivot

There was silence. Then Lexi said, "It's a better story."

Raj shrugged. "It's riskier. But cooler."

Niko sighed, then smirked. "Fine. But only because parking apps are boring."

They pivoted hard. Scrapped the algorithm. Built a clean, mobile-first interface called "New Pathway."

It used simple geolocation to connect users to nearby free tech literacy events, Wi-Fi hotspots, device donation programs, and digital application guides, partnered with libraries and nonprofits.

They designed it with a minimal interface. No jargon. Large text. One-click navigation.

It wasn't flashy.

But it worked.

The Pitch Room

By Sunday afternoon, their team stood on the makeshift stage with thirty other teams. Some pitched blockchain logistics. Others had AI tutors or smart fridge integrations.

When it was their turn, Ava stepped up.

She didn't open with data.

She opened with a story.

"Last year, my grandma had to walk six blocks in the rain to apply for housing online. The library computer timed out. She had to come back the next day. That's what digital exclusion looks like."

Then she showed New Pathway, highlighting who it was for much more than its capabilities.

When they stepped off stage, she didn't know if they'd win.

But they'd built something that mattered.

What Came After

They didn't take first place.

They took *second*. And more importantly? A rep from the San Jose Public Library came up after the pitch.

"This is what we've been needing. Can we talk about piloting it at our East Branch?"

Ava blinked. "Seriously?"

He nodded. "No one's building for our seniors. But you did."

Skill: Adaptability

✅ Changing direction isn't quitting; it's evolving with purpose.

✅ The smartest people aren't the ones with a perfect plan. They're the ones who adapt to real needs.

✅ Let go of your ego and listen to what the moment is asking for.

~

Practice the Skill: Adaptability

1. The "Flip It" Exercise

Take one personal or school project you've already started. Then ask:

If I had to pivot this in a new direction, with the same tools, what could I build instead?

Challenge yourself to brainstorm two to three fresh uses for your existing work.

Why it works: It trains your brain to see potential, not just problems, and shows you that nothing is ever truly wasted.

2. Choose the Curveball

For one week, intentionally pick the *second-best* option in your routine:

> Take a new route to class.
>
> Use a different productivity app.
>
> Sit in a new spot in the cafeteria or library.

Then jot down: What did you learn? What was uncomfortable? What surprised you?

Why it works: Small disruptions build the muscle of flexibility, so you're stronger when real change comes.

3. Run a "Post-Mortem" on a Past Pivot

Think back to a time when a plan didn't go the way you hoped at school, work, or even socially.

Now ask yourself:

> What changed?
>
> How did I respond?
>
> What would I do differently next time?

Write a short reflection, like a mini case study of your own adaptability journey.

Why it works: Reflection turns experience into growth and gives you a playbook for the next pivot.

CHAPTER 13:
THE MIRROR MOMENT

"You can't fix what you won't face. And you can't lead what you won't listen to."

Fordham University – Bronx, NYC

The stained-glass windows of Keating Hall glowed with late afternoon light as Dani adjusted her slides for the capstone marketing project. Outside, the Bronx rumbled with its usual city symphony–sirens, sidewalk chatter, and a food truck hawking empanadas. Inside, Room 213 buzzed with group tension.

They were three weeks into the semester-long campaign project for their senior seminar at Fordham, and Dani had become the unofficial captain of their four-person team. Not by vote. Just by volume.

She double-checked the deck she had finished at 2 a.m. the night before. Color-coded sections. Market research graphs. Strategic rollout plan.

It was sharp. It was polished.

And she'd barely let anyone else touch it.

The Feedback She Didn't Expect

Josh, a communications major with a calm voice and a coffee-stained notebook, spoke up after class.

"Hey, can we talk?" he asked, motioning toward the hallway.

Dani followed, still holding her laptop. "What's up?"

Josh exhaled. "Look, you're clearly invested. But I think it's hard for the rest of us to contribute."

Dani blinked. "I just want to make sure we turn in something great."

"I know," Josh said, gently. "But it's like we're not even on the team. You redo slides, rewrite our copy ... even our ideas kind of vanish."

The words stung. She opened her mouth to defend herself but stopped.

"I'm only bringing it up because I think it matters," Josh added. "I just thought you should know."

She nodded stiffly. "Thanks for telling me."

The Late Walk and the Long Reflection

That evening, Dani went for a walk. The city buzz was louder now—horns, laughter, the hum of the D Train pulling into Fordham Road Station. She stopped at a bench under a maple tree and opened her phone's Notes app.

CHAPTER 13: THE MIRROR MOMENT

Her last group project in high school had bombed. She'd trusted others to carry their weight. They hadn't. She got burned and vowed never to let that happen again.

But now? She realized she'd gone too far the other way.

She wasn't leading. She was taking over.

And it wasn't helping anyone.

The Shift in Approach

At their next team meeting in the McGinley Center lounge, Dani arrived early with a surprise. No slides, just snacks. And four fresh notebooks.

"Okay," she said, "I've been doing too much. I want this to be a real collaboration. Let's start from scratch together."

Josh raised an eyebrow. Mia looked relieved. Andre smiled and said, "Took you long enough."

They redivided the work. Mia ran interviews. Josh designed visuals. Andre crafted the social media strategy. Dani stuck to editing and logistics and learned to ask before offering feedback.

It wasn't perfect. She slipped once, tweaking Josh's layout without asking. He called her out. She apologized. They moved on.

The Presentation That Landed

The day of the final pitch, they stood side by side in front of their classmates and a panel of industry mentors. Their campaign for a local Bronx bookstore was vibrant, data-backed, and rooted in authentic neighborhood storytelling.

Mia opened. Josh walked through visuals. Dani took the Q&A.

Afterward, their professor approached. "Best teamwork I've seen all semester," she said. "You played to each other's strengths."

Later that night, Dani sat by the Lincoln Center fountain downtown, watching the lights ripple across the water.

She didn't just feel proud of the grade.

She felt proud of the growth.

Skill:
Self-Awareness

☑ You can't change a pattern you won't admit.

☑ Knowing how others experience you is a form of wisdom, not weakness.

☑ Great teammates (and leaders) take feedback personally, in the best way.

~

Practice the Skill: Self-Awareness

💬 1. Run the "Mirror Test" After a Group Project

After your next group collaboration (class, internship, or club), ask yourself:

What did I contribute most?

Where might I have overstepped or under-showed?

How did people respond to my energy, tone, or pace?

Why it works: Self-awareness grows when you reflect *after* the fact, not just in the moment. This helps you notice patterns in how you show up.

📣 2. Ask for Feedback with a Twist

Instead of asking, "How did I do?" try:

"What's one thing I did that helped the team?"

"What's one thing I could shift next time?"

Why it works: Framing feedback as specific and two-sided makes people more honest and makes you more open.

✎ 3. Map Your Strengths and Blind Spots

Draw two columns on a page:
Left side = *Things I do well in groups.*
Right side = *Things I tend to overdo or forget.*

Be honest. Add to it over time. Use it before new projects.

Why it works: Awareness isn't just knowing your strengths; it's knowing when they become liabilities.

CHAPTER 14: THE LESSON IN THE LOBBY

"Professionalism isn't what you wear to the interview. It's how you carry yourself before it even begins."

Downtown Chicago – Spring Wind, Sharp Lessons

Micah Wells zipped up his coat against the gusts swirling through the Loop. He crossed under the L and passed the Wabash Avenue Starbucks, doing a final check: blazer pressed, portfolio folder zipped, tie straight. This was it, his first interview at a downtown firm.

The company was called Bryant & Moss, a midsize consulting firm known for its Gen Z-friendly branding and strong social impact division. He'd been researching them since winter break, dreaming of the internship program that had launched dozens of undergrads into careers.

Micah was a junior at DePaul, majoring in Business Strategy and minoring in Public Policy. He had worked part-time retail, led a case competition, and even helped his aunt build out the Shopify for her candle business. This internship was a chance to prove he belonged in boardrooms, not just backrooms.

He arrived fifteen minutes early like every article had said to. As he stepped into the sleek, high-rise lobby of the River West building, he spotted someone at the front desk in joggers, a zip-up hoodie, and AirPods.

Micah gave him a quick nod.

"Morning," the guy said.

Micah offered a faint "Hey" but kept walking toward the row of elevators, focused on reviewing his mental script.

The Girl with the Red Backpack

Near the seating area, a young woman in a maroon blazer adjusted her heels and glanced at her phone. She had a red backpack instead of a briefcase, which made Micah feel less underdressed.

"You here for the Bryant & Moss thing?" she asked.

"Yeah, strategy intern," Micah replied.

"Same," she smiled. "I'm Naila. UChicago."

"Micah. DePaul."

They made small talk—majors, professors, the chaos of balancing work and class.

Then she asked, "What did you think of Theo?"

Micah blinked. "I haven't met him yet."

Naila tilted her head. "That was him at the desk. In the hoodie. He leads the intern program."

Micah felt his stomach drop.

CHAPTER 14: THE LESSON IN THE LOBBY

"That was Theo Bell?" he whispered.

Naila nodded. "Yeah. I said hi earlier. He was talking about a campaign he just wrapped." She paused. "Did you talk to him?"

Micah winced. "I kind of … didn't. I thought he was a delivery guy or something."

Naila raised an eyebrow, then offered a shrug that suggested: *Yikes, but maybe not too late.*

The Interview That Was Already in Progress

Micah was eventually called upstairs to a glass conference room that overlooked the river. Across the table sat Theo, now in a button-up, and a senior associate named Rachel.

Theo didn't mention the lobby.

The interview was fine, solid even. Micah had good answers, thoughtful takes on Bryant & Moss's latest campaign, and strong examples from his coursework.

But something felt off. Theo's responses were brief. Polite. Neutral.

The kind of energy that said: *This isn't personal. But it is professional.*

The Email That Shifted Everything

Micah didn't get the offer.

But five days later, an email landed in his inbox with the subject line:

"Feedback That Might Help"

> Micah,
>
> I appreciate your preparation and ideas. You're clearly smart and have a great attitude.
>
> One thing I'll offer as feedback, not to discourage, but to help:
>
> Professionalism isn't just what you say in the meeting. It's what you do in the in-between.
>
> The lobby matters. The small moments matter. People remember how you treat everyone, especially when you don't know who they are yet.
>
> Hope this helps as you move forward. You've got potential.
>
> – Theo

Micah read it twice. Three times.

It wasn't cold. It wasn't cruel.

It was a mirror.

What Changed

He printed the email, taped it inside his notebook, then got to work. He wasn't simply focusing on résumé bullet points, but how he moved through the world.

He started with small things.

CHAPTER 14: THE LESSON IN THE LOBBY

👋 Saying good morning to the janitor at his campus job.

📅 Showing up ten minutes early to group projects prepared, not rushed.

💬 Responding to emails with more clarity.

📝 Offering to take notes in team meetings.

🎯 Treating every moment like it was already part of the interview.

When he applied to another internship a month later, this time with a fintech company in the West Loop, he recognized the hiring manager before the meeting even started. It was the woman who had helped him navigate the firm's glitchy portal earlier that week. He thanked her by name before stepping into the room.

This time, he got the offer.

Skill: Professionalism

✅ Being prepared isn't just about your résumé; it's about your presence.

✅ Respect begins with how you treat everyone, not just decision-makers.

✅ Professionalism is a habit, not a performance.

∼

Practice the Skill: Professionalism

🎯 1. The "Every Space Is a Stage" Challenge

For one full week, treat every setting, classroom, email thread, group chat, elevator, campus job, as a place where your professionalism is quietly observed.

Ask yourself: *Would I be proud if someone important saw this moment?*

Why it works: It trains your consistency. People decide if you're trustworthy in the hallway, not just in the interview room.

🧠 2. Write Your Professional Standards

List 3–5 specific ways you want to show up professionally this semester. Example:

    Show up 10 minutes early to everything.

    Use complete sentences in emails.

    Greet people by name, especially staff.

Why it works: Professionalism becomes personal when it's defined on your terms, not just your résumé.

📓 3. Reflect on a Missed Moment

Think of a time when you *didn't* show up the way you wanted to. Maybe you were late, dismissive, unprepared, or too casual. Write what you'd do differently now. Then forgive yourself and move forward.

Why it works: Growth comes from reflection, not regret. Self-awareness is a core part of professionalism.

CHAPTER 15:
THE DAY THAT GOT AWAY

*"Time doesn't disappear, it gets spent.
Make sure you're the one doing the spending."*

San Diego State University – Midterm Season, Caffeine, and Chaos

Tyler knew what overwhelm felt like. But this? This was something else. The calendar on his dorm wall, marked in multicolored dry-erase scribbles, looked more like an abstract painting than a plan. Marketing midterm. Club event prep. Freelance video edit. Internship application. Pickup game. Group project. Student senate notes. His own birthday dinner, somewhat lost amidst it all.

His laptop blinked with notifications. His phone buzzed nonstop. His AirPods were in, but no music played. And his mind? Racing.

He sat on the floor of his dorm, surrounded by open textbooks, a half-drunk iced coffee, a crumpled to-do list, and his half-charged planner.

"I just need one focused hour," he whispered to himself.

He opened his notes for tomorrow's poli-sci class, determined to start. But before he could highlight a single sentence, his group chat lit up:

"You coming to set up for tonight's speaker panel?"

"Client's asking for final edits by 8!"

"Yo, we still playing at 6:30?"

Tyler stared at his phone then at the wall clock: 5:21 p.m.

He hadn't done a single thing on his to-do list. And now it was too late to do any of it well.

The Collapse, In Real Time

By 6:30 p.m., Tyler was jogging to the rec center.

By 8:15, he was scarfing down a breakfast burrito from the taco truck outside Love Library, still in his gym clothes.

By 9:00, he was back in his room, trying to salvage the client video edit.

At 9:22, the email came in:

"Thanks for trying, but we're going with someone else this time."

By 10:05, he remembered the event wrap-up slides he was supposed to finish.

And at 10:37, his roommate walked in to find Tyler face down in his open econ textbook.

He wasn't lazy. He wasn't unmotivated.

He just couldn't outrun his own day.

CHAPTER 15: THE DAY THAT GOT AWAY

The Coffee Napkin Blueprint

Two mornings later, Tyler met Shayna at West Commons Café.

Shayna, a junior in environmental policy, had a rep around campus: organized, unflustered, everywhere at once and still early to class. She ran the sustainability club, interned at the city council office, had a 3.8 GPA, and somehow remembered everyone's name.

Tyler slumped into his seat. "I think I broke my brain."

Shayna sipped her tea. "Did your Google Calendar betray you again?"

He nodded. "I plan it all out. I color-code everything. But my days just ... collapse. Like a folding chair in a hurricane."

Shayna smiled. "Then you're doing time management backwards."

Tyler blinked. "How?"

"You're stuffing your day like a suitcase and hoping nothing explodes. But time doesn't bend. It breaks." She grabbed a napkin and drew three boxes.

Must-Do. Should-Do. Can-Wait.

"Every day, I ask: What's the one thing I'll be proud I did today? That's your *Must-Do*. Then you layer on the *Should-Dos*, stuff that helps but isn't mission critical. And the rest? It waits."

Tyler stared at the napkin.

"I call it the Time Budget," she said. "You get 24 dollars a day. You decide what to spend them on. If you overspend, you pay in stress and missed chances."

The Struggle to Reset

That night, Tyler sat on his bed with his laptop open, planner beside him.

He tried the napkin method.

Must-Do:

> Finish final cut for nonprofit client.
>
> Study 45 minutes for econ quiz.
>
> Text his sister back about their grandma's surgery.

Should-Do:

> Work on the senate proposal.
>
> Brainstorm next week's club agenda.
>
> Go to the gym.

Can-Wait:

> Update his YouTube thumbnails.
>
> Design new merch for his video series.
>
> Watch the latest Lakers game highlights.

It didn't feel perfect. But it felt ... clearer.

He still had to say no to things. Still had to disappoint people. Still caught himself scrolling when he promised he'd focus.

But the next day? He hit all his Must-Dos.

CHAPTER 15: THE DAY THAT GOT AWAY

The day after? He added a twenty minute walk break and finally had space to think.

By the end of the week? He submitted his internship application early, with a portfolio that didn't make him cringe.

One Month Later, A Different Day

Tyler stood outside the study hall, chatting with the head of SDSU's communications program. She'd just reviewed his application for a summer fellowship.

"You've really stepped up your game," she said. "Your references had great things to say, especially about how consistent and reliable you've been."

Tyler smiled. Not because he was the most productive guy on campus. But because, for the first time, he was in charge of his own time, and not just reacting to it.

Skill:
Time Management

☑ **Time mastery isn't about doing everything. It's about doing the right things deliberately.**

☑ **You don't "find" time. *You budget* it.**

☑ **Focus is the new flex. Build it like a muscle.**

∼

Practice the Skill: Time Management

1. Build Your "Time Budget" Daily

Every night or morning, divide your tasks into three categories:

Must-Do (non-negotiables: class, work deadlines, health)

Should-Do (important but flexible: studying, check-ins, organizing)

Can-Wait (bonus stuff: design tweaks, deep cleaning)

Then, assign time blocks (with breaks!) to each.

Example:

Must-Do: 1 hr studying, 30 min gym, 1 hr project

Should-Do: prep slides, clean room

Can-Wait: edit TikTok, watch new show

Why it works: It helps you prioritize what truly matters *before* distractions take over.

⏰ 2. Track Your Time Like Money, for One Day

Use your phone notes, calendar, or a free app to track how you spend every hour of your day, from waking up to bedtime.

Then ask:

> What did I spend the most time on?
>
> Did it match my priorities?
>
> Where did I lose time to distractions?

Why it works: Awareness is power. You can't fix what you don't track.

🚫 3. Make a "NO List"

Time management isn't just about what you do; it's also about what you *stop* doing.

Make a list of 3 things you'll say no to this week, things that drain time or pull you off track.

Example:

✗ Checking social media before 9 a.m.
✗ Saying yes to every group hang
✗ Multitasking while studying

Why it works: Time is finite. Saying *no* creates space for what deserves your *yes*.

CHAPTER 16: TAMING THE SPIRAL

"Time doesn't move faster when you're behind, only louder."

Seattle, Washington - The Internship of Her Dreams, And Her Dread

Lena had always known her brain worked differently. At first, it felt like a superpower. She could connect dots no one else saw, create wild, scroll-stopping ideas in seconds, and dream up slogans with the punch of poetry. In high school, her sketchbooks were filled with campaign pitches for fictional products, like eco-friendly cereal or vegan nail polish.

Now, at twenty, she was finally in the world she used to imagine: Cal Anderson Creative, a boutique marketing agency in Seattle's Capitol Hill known for bold design and brand strategy that walked the line between edgy and ethical.

She had earned the internship fair and square through a competitive portfolio review, a group interview, and a wildly creative prompt ("Pitch a product launch for a glow-in-the-dark umbrella").

And she'd nailed it.

But now, one week in, Lena was spiraling. Again.

The Ping-Pong Brain Problem

Her desk overlooked a moss-covered mural alley. Across the room, copywriters huddled around an espresso cart someone had rolled in as a Friday "brainstorm boost." Music played softly from a shared Spotify playlist. Someone's dog wandered around in a Seahawks jersey.

It should've been perfect.

But Lena was drowning.

A Slack ping would knock her out of focus. She'd open a brief to check a logo spec then suddenly find herself two tabs deep into unrelated email threads. Halfway through a mood board, she'd remember she hadn't responded to a client comment. Then she'd panic, open five more tabs, and start doom-scrolling fonts. By lunch, nothing was finished, and her stomach was in knots.

"I'm so disorganized," she muttered under her breath, stabbing at her sandwich in the break room.

Across the table, Brielle, a senior strategist with turquoise box braids and a calm, commanding vibe, looked up.

"You're not disorganized," Brielle said. "You're just not working with your brain. Yet."

Lena blinked. "Sorry?"

Brielle smiled. "Been there. ADHD?"

Lena hesitated, then nodded. "Diagnosed last year."

"Same. Come with me."

Three Tools from a Fellow Spiral-Survivor

Brielle brought her to a quiet conference room with a whiteboard and a couch.

"Everyone says, 'just make a to-do list.' But for us, that's like giving a GPS to someone in a tornado," she said. "You need tools that *interrupt the spiral.*"

She wrote on the board:

1. The Parking Lot

"Every time your brain tries to yank you into another task, jot it down here. That idea? That worry? That reminder to text someone back? Park it. Don't lose it, just don't follow it. You get one 'parking lot' per work block. Review it after."

2. Visual Blocking

Brielle opened a doc: a daily calendar broken into color-coded boxes. But instead of vague task names, it had things like "Design Hero Image (30 min, no email)," "Snack + walk," and "Admin Hour (batch all Slack replies)."

"I block for energy, not time," Brielle said. "And I design my day like a playlist."

3. The Win Wall

She pointed to sticky notes on the far wall.

"Every time you complete something, no matter how small, write it down and stick it up. Watch what happens to your self-esteem."

Lena stared. "This is … genius."

Brielle laughed. "It's survival. Let me know if you want the templates."

Implementation: From Spiral to System

Back at her desk, Lena started small.

She opened a new tab titled "Parking Lot" and added:

Fix colors on Brand Brew deck

Email Jules about the workshop

Look up new fonts (NOT NOW!)

Then she opened a doc called "Today's Playlist" and created blocks:

🎧 10:00–10:30: Mood board edits (headphones, no Slack)

💦 10:30–10:45: Water break + check Parking Lot

✉ 10:45–11:30: Emails + questions for Brielle

By lunch, three things were actually finished. She wrote them on sticky notes and stuck them on her monitor:

- ✔ Finalized social concepts for Hydrate.
- ✔ Sent revised CTA copy.
- ✔ Didn't spiral.

She smiled.

For the first time that week, her body didn't feel like it was bracing for a tidal wave.

What Came After

Two weeks later, Lena led the creative pitch for a new client: a local zero-waste store launching its first e-commerce platform.

Her mood board was tight. Her concept sketches sang. Her delivery was calm and grounded.

Afterward, Brielle caught her in the hallway.

"Didn't spiral," she said with a wink.

"Playlist mode," Lena replied.

Skill:
Time Management
(with a Creative, ADHD-Friendly Brain)

☑ **If you keep losing focus, your system, not your worth, needs tweaking.**

☑ **The right tools don't just help you finish; they help you breathe.**

☑ **Managing time isn't about becoming someone else. It's about designing your day like it's built *for you*.**

∼

🦴 Practice the Skill: Time Management for Creative, Neurodivergent Minds

🧠 1. Build a "Parking Lot" Distraction Tracker

Create a digital note, whiteboard column, or sticky note labeled "Parking Lot." Every time a non-urgent thought, task, or idea pops up while you're focused on something else, jot it there.

Review it at a designated break, not in the middle of your task.

Why it works: It honors your brain's ideas without letting them hijack your focus.

🎨 2. Design a Time "Playlist" Instead of a Schedule

Break your day into twenty-five to forty-five minute time blocks, each labeled by *mood*, *energy*, or *type of thinking*.

Examples:

> 🎧 "Solo Build Mode" (no interruptions, headphones on)
>
> ☕ "Admin + Email Time" (low energy, batch tasks)
>
> 🌿 "Recharge Block" (movement, snacks, water)

Why it works: Creative minds resist rigid structure. This adds rhythm without pressure.

3. Start a Win Wall

Keep a visible note board or digital list where you record completed tasks, no matter how small.

At the end of each day, reflect on what you *did* instead of what you didn't.

Why it works: Dopamine matters. Seeing your progress builds momentum and self-trust.

CHAPTER 17:
THE PERSPECTIVE THAT CHANGED EVERYTHING

"Empathy isn't about fixing. It's about seeing."

Lewis & Clark College – Portland, Oregon

Emery had color-coded highlighters, a resume that already had three bullet points under "Community Impact," and a desk calendar that mapped out her semester week by week. She wasn't just organized; she was mission driven.

That's why she joined Pathway, the mentorship initiative connecting college students with local high schoolers navigating the college application process. Helping people had always been her thing.

Plus, it didn't hurt that the leadership team for Pathway included upperclassmen who had interned at Teach for America, launched voter registration drives, and landed fellowships Emery secretly bookmarked.

She had goals.

She had a system.

What she didn't have yet was perspective.

The First Meeting That Didn't Go as Planned

Tara, one of Emery's assigned mentees from Roosevelt High, showed up to their first Zoom call five minutes late. Her camera was off.

Emery launched into her usual intro:

"Hey! So, I thought we'd walk through your Common App timeline today. If we start now, we can get your essay draft done by mid-October, then you'll have room to revise and submit an early decision."

No response.

"…Tara?"

A moment later: "Yeah. Sorry. I'm here. Just… rough day."

Emery smiled, even though the silence on the other end felt awkward. "No worries! We'll keep it quick."

They didn't get far. Tara mumbled a few answers, left a few blanks in the intake worksheet, and signed off early with, "I'll try to look at this stuff later."

Emery stared at the screen after it went dark.

She checked the box next to *Initial Meeting* in her tracker, but something didn't sit right.

The Wrong Kind of Progress

A week passed. No replies to emails. No submission of the personal statement outline.

Emery vented during the next Pathway staff huddle in the student lounge, rain streaking the windows and the smell of cinnamon muffins in the air.

"I just don't get it," she said to Jon, her team lead. "We give them resources, structure, everything. Some of them still don't take it seriously."

Jon didn't scold her. He just stirred his coffee and said, "Sometimes what looks like disinterest is actually a defense. Silence is communication, too."

Emery blinked. "So, what do I do? Just stop following up?"

"No. You shift how you show up."

The Shift in Approach

That night, Emery sat in her dorm room, rain still tapping the windows, her roommate humming to Phoebe Bridgers in the background. She reread her emails to Tara. They were structured, cheerful, goal oriented.

But they weren't human.

So, she wrote something different. Something that didn't have a checklist attached.

Subject: I've Been Thinking About You

> Hey Tara,
>
> I just wanted to say, I see you. Not your GPA. Not your deadlines. You. If you ever want to talk about anything, college, life, your day, I'm here. No pressure, no expectations.
>
> I'm learning that showing up means more than staying on schedule. So, I'm starting over.
>
> You don't owe me a reply.
> But I'm holding space for you.
>
> Emery

What Came Back

Tara replied three days later. It wasn't long.

> Thanks. I'm just trying to keep my mom stable and hold down my job. College stuff got too loud. But your message helped. I'll reach out when I can.

They met the next week at a corner café off MLK Boulevard. Tara ordered green tea and kept her hoodie up.

"I thought if I admitted how hard things are, it would sound like I don't care about my future," she said. "But I do. I just don't have a lot of room to show it."

Emery nodded. "I didn't ask that before. I'm sorry."

From that point forward, their meetings changed.

Emery started with, "What do you need this week?"

CHAPTER 17: THE PERSPECTIVE THAT CHANGED EVERYTHING

She listened more. Asked better questions. She helped Tara find a college counselor through Pathway's community network who specialized in first-gen applicants.

They built a real connection. One that didn't rely on bullet points or timelines.

What Came After

At the end-of-year Pathway gathering, Tara stood up to speak.

She talked about her acceptance to Portland State. About keeping her job. About writing her essay late at night while her mom slept on the couch beside her.

And then she looked at Emery and said, "You didn't ask me to show up perfect. You showed up real. That helped me believe I belonged."

Emery looked around the room at all the mentees, the mentors, the messy applications and long-shot dreams, and finally understood.

Empathy wasn't about fixing. It was about seeing.

And being seen.

Skill: Empathy

☑ **Listening without judgment builds trust faster than any plan.**

☑ **People don't always need answers. Sometimes they just need to know they're not alone.**

☑ **Empathy shifts everything, from how we lead to how we show up.**

~

Practice the Skill: Empathy

1. Listen Like It's Your Job

Pick a conversation this week where your goal is not to respond or solve, but to fully *listen*. Try this rule:

> No interrupting.
>
> Ask one follow-up question before you respond.
>
> Pause before offering advice.

Why it works: Most people listen to *reply*. Empathic listeners listen to *understand*. That small shift builds connection fast.

2. Write a Message Without an Ask

Reach out to someone in your life—a classmate, coworker, mentee, or friend—and send a message that has *no agenda*. Just encouragement, acknowledgement, or support.

Example:

"Hey, I know this week's been a lot. Just wanted to say I'm proud of how you're showing up. No need to reply, just rooting for you."

Why it works: Empathy doesn't always show up in conversation. It shows up in care that expects nothing back.

CHAPTER 17: THE PERSPECTIVE THAT CHANGED EVERYTHING

☺ 3. Flip the Frustration

The next time someone's response frustrates you–slow email, silence, disengagement, pause and ask:

"What might they be carrying that I can't see?"

"What's a kinder interpretation of this moment?"

Why it works: Reframing assumptions helps you respond with compassion instead of judgment, which keeps relationships open and supportive.

CHAPTER 18: THE LINE SHE CHOSE TO HOLD

"Integrity is doing the right thing, especially when no one's watching and it would be easier not to."

Asheville, North Carolina – The Mist and the Mission

The early October fog still clung to the Blue Ridge Mountains as Sasha crossed the quad at UNC Asheville, hot tea in one hand and laptop bag slung across her shoulder. She exhaled a cloud of breath into the crisp morning and made her way toward the student innovation hub, a glass-walled building tucked near the edge of campus known for late nights, big ideas, and even bigger caffeine habits.

Inside, her team was prepping for the final round of the Blue Ridge Social Impact Pitch Competition. Their project, MountainCare Connect, was a mobile app designed to connect rural and low-income residents with affordable health resources across western North Carolina. The idea had started as a class brainstorm, but Sasha had driven it forward, largely inspired by her mom, a home health nurse who'd spent years zigzagging through backroads and waiting rooms.

Winning this competition meant funding. Mentorship. Visibility. Sasha could already see the line on her resume, "Co-founder, MountainCare Connect", and the interview nods it would bring.

She sat down and opened the pitch deck. That's when she saw it.

The Mistake That Meant Everything

Slide 12: "Impact So Far."

The numbers looked incredible. 750 users in the first month. 89% reported improved access to care. 120+ referrals to local providers.

Except... it wasn't real.

They were projected figures from a scenario model Jay had built. Mia must have pulled the wrong slide version. Or maybe just assumed they were from the pilot they'd discussed but never launched.

Sasha stared at the numbers, her stomach tightening.

If left unchanged, the judges would assume MountainCare Connect had already been field-tested. That they weren't just pitching a good idea but proving results.

Her cursor hovered over the delete key.

What if we just left it? she thought. *We didn't say it was real. If no one asks...*

But even as the thought flickered, her gut answered.

That's not how you want to win.

CHAPTER 18: THE LINE SHE CHOSE TO HOLD

The Conversation That Could've Gone Either Way

The team met that afternoon in a study room in Ramsey Library. Sasha waited until they'd run through the deck once, then cleared her throat.

"I need to flag something," she said, turning her laptop toward them.

Jay leaned forward. Mia crossed her arms.

"These numbers, on slide twelve, they're our projections. We haven't launched the pilot yet. But the way it's phrased … it looks like we have."

There was a pause. A long one.

Jay winced. "Oh wow. That's my model. I didn't think we were putting it in like that."

Mia didn't speak for a moment. "But we *plan* to hit those numbers. They're not fake."

"No," Sasha agreed. "They're not fake. But they're not real yet either. And if we let people believe they are, that's not just a stretch, it's a misrepresentation."

Mia looked frustrated. "But those numbers make us look credible. If we take them out, we're just another group with a good idea and no traction."

Sasha nodded. "I get that. I do. But if we win with this version, we're winning with something we haven't actually done. I'd rather lose being honest than win by misleading."

The silence stretched again. Then Jay nodded. "She's right."

Mia sighed. "Fine. But we need to reframe the slide or we're going to sound weak."

"We'll tell the truth," Sasha said. "And we'll make the vision strong enough to stand on its own."

The Pitch That Didn't Impress Everyone But Did Matter

The final round took place in a sleek coworking space downtown, full of reclaimed wood and Edison bulbs. Investors and community leaders filled the seats. The Blue Ridge Mountains peeked through the windows like silent judges.

Sasha took a breath and stepped up with her team.

When they reached the impact slide, she held the clicker a beat longer.

"These are our *projected* outcomes," she said. "They come from models based on local health access data with support from our community health partners. We haven't launched MountainCare Connect yet. But we've done the groundwork. These are the results we plan to deliver, and we're ready to make them real."

There were fewer nods than she'd hoped. One judge scribbled something and frowned. Another didn't react at all.

But after the presentations, a woman with silver braids approached them. She introduced herself as a community health director from Buncombe County.

"I appreciated the honesty," she said. "It's rare. If you're looking for a launch partner, call me."

CHAPTER 18: THE LINE SHE CHOSE TO HOLD

What Comes Next

They didn't win the prize.

But the email that arrived a week later with the subject line "Let's Pilot MountainCare Connect" felt like something better.

And Mia? She texted Sasha two days after that.

"I was mad at first. But you were right. Thanks for holding the line."

Sasha saved the message. Not for her résumé.

For her *mirror*.

Skill: Integrity

✅ Integrity means saying "not yet" instead of pretending "already."

✅ Doing the right thing may not always win applause, but it earns trust.

✅ Long-term impact isn't built on perfect slides. It's built on truth.

～

🦴 Practice the Skill: Integrity

🧪 1. "Would I Say This in a Room of Experts?" Check

Before you pitch an idea, post a stat, or share an accomplishment, ask yourself:

Would I say this in a room where everyone knows the truth?

If the answer is "not really" or "I'd have to hedge," revise your claim until it's clear and honest, even if it's less flashy.

Why it works: It keeps you grounded and credible, especially when you're building a reputation.

💬 2. Rehearse the Hard Truth

Write a short script (two to three sentences) for how you would speak up if you caught something misleading in a group project, campaign, or presentation. Example:

"Hey, I noticed we said we already launched, but it's actually just in development. I think we should clarify so we don't misrepresent ourselves."

Practice saying it out loud, alone, or with a trusted friend.

Why it works: Speaking up is easier when you've rehearsed the hard conversations first.

🔍 3. Track Your Tiny Truths

Start a private "Integrity Journal" on your phone or notebook. Once a week, jot down one moment where:

> You could've stretched the truth but didn't.

> You admitted a mistake, even when no one else noticed.

> You asked for a correction or clarification to keep things accurate.

Why it works: Integrity isn't just big moral moments; it's built in daily micro-decisions.

CHAPTER 19: THE CONNECTION AT THE SIGN-IN TABLE

*"You don't have to chase opportunities.
Just show up ready and be worth remembering."*

Los Angeles, California – Saturday Evening, 6:17 p.m.

Evan adjusted the stack of name tags for the fifth time, checking them against the printout on his clipboard. Around him, the ballroom at the Los Angeles Convention Center shimmered under soft lighting. Waitstaff moved quietly between high-top tables with trays of canapés, and a jazz trio played near the stage.

This was the NextSteps annual fundraising event for a local nonprofit that helped high schoolers from underserved communities break into tech. Evan, a sophomore computer science major at the University of Southern California, had started volunteering with them earlier in the semester, running basic coding workshops on Saturdays. It wasn't fancy, but it felt like something that mattered.

Tonight, he was working the sign-in table.

He didn't think much of it. Honestly, he'd volunteered because he needed service hours for a leadership class, and because they said there'd be cupcakes.

But as the line started to form, Evan felt the pressure settle in. Suits. Blazers. Laughter that sounded expensive. Everyone here seemed important.

He tugged at his borrowed button-down and did his best to look like he belonged.

A Calm Voice in the Crowd

"Need an extra set of hands?" a voice asked beside him.

Evan turned. A tall man in dark jeans and a hoodie with the logo Frontier 52 AI Lab stood beside the table, already sorting a second stack of lanyards.

"Uh, sure, yeah," Evan said. "Thanks."

The guy's name tag read "Jordan M.–Board Member."

Jordan worked quickly and quietly. Within minutes, they were operating like a machine–Evan on the printed list and Jordan on the tablet. As people came through, Jordan greeted them with a relaxed confidence that made everyone feel welcome. He cracked a quiet joke when someone forgot their RSVP, handed out extra programs, and never missed a beat.

Evan tried to match his pace. He didn't know Jordan's title, he assumed maybe marketing or operations, but it was clear he knew how to run things.

CHAPTER 19: THE CONNECTION AT THE SIGN-IN TABLE

The RSVP That Went Off-Script

A woman in a navy jumpsuit approached, clearly annoyed.

"My name's not on the list?" she asked, incredulous. "That's not possible, I registered last week."

Evan scanned the page again. Still nothing. His stomach flipped. She was already looking around like she wanted to talk to someone higher up.

"I'm really sorry about this," he said, his voice steady. "We've had some issues with the RSVP system tonight. Let me make this right."

He pulled out a blank tag, wrote her name neatly, added a handwritten "Welcome!" at the bottom, and handed it to her with a smile.

"You're all set. Thank you for your patience, I'll make sure the team updates the list for next year, so this doesn't happen again."

The woman blinked. Then nodded, slightly disarmed. "Okay. Thanks."

As she walked off, Jordan glanced over.

"You've got poise," he said. "That could've gone sideways fast."

Evan shrugged. "I work in a coffee shop near campus. Handling grumpy customers is half the shift."

Jordan smiled. "Good training."

The Surprise at the End of the Shift

As the guest flow slowed and they packed up the extras, they made small talk. Evan told Jordan he was studying computer science and trying to figure out if he wanted to go into design, software, or something in between.

"Something that makes life easier for people," he added. "I'm sometimes not even sure how to get my foot in the door. Tech jobs feel kind of... untouchable."

Jordan raised an eyebrow. "Not if you're already the kind of person people want to work with."

Then he reached into his pocket and handed Evan a card.

Jordan Martin

CEO | Frontier 52 AI Lab

Evan stared. "You're the CEO?"

Jordan chuckled. "I don't usually lead with that."

The Email That Took Thirty Minutes to Write

Back in his apartment, Evan stared at the card for a full minute before pulling up his email.

He drafted five versions of the message before finally sending:

CHAPTER 19: THE CONNECTION AT THE SIGN-IN TABLE

Subject: Great Working with You at the Gala

> Hi Jordan,
>
> Thanks again for your help at the check-in table. I really enjoyed the event, and appreciated how calm you kept things even when it got hectic.
>
> I checked out Frontier 52 AI Lab, what you're building looks awesome. If there's ever a way I can contribute or learn more, I'd love to stay in touch.
>
> Evan Taylor
>
> USC '27 | Computer Science

He hit send, then immediately questioned every word.

The Reply That Opened a Door

The next morning, Jordan responded:

> Evan,
>
> You handled last night with more professionalism than people twice your age. People skills matter just as much as tech skills, sometimes more.
>
> Stay in touch. Keep me posted on your journey. You've got something.
>
> Jordan

Three Months Later

Finals were over. Evan had built a small web app as part of his software design course and started dabbling in UX during his downtime. He remembered Jordan's words and decided to email a short update.

Subject: Semester Update

> Hi Jordan,
>
> Just wanted to share a quick update. Finished finals, took Web Design and Databases, and built a budgeting tool for my design project. Learned a lot.
>
> Hope things are going well at Frontier 52 AI Lab!
>
> Evan

An hour later, Jordan replied:

> Let's chat. I've got a summer internship with your name on it, if you're interested.
>
> You earned this.

Skill: Networking, Even When You're Not "Networking"

☑ You don't need a conference or résumé to network, you need presence and people skills.

☑ Follow-up shows interest and builds trust.

☑ Great impressions are made in ordinary moments.

Practice the Skill: Networking (Without Feeling Cringe)

🤝 1. Start Where You Are

You don't have to be at a career fair to network. Look around: who do you meet at volunteer events, campus orgs, or part-time jobs? Introduce yourself, ask thoughtful questions, and share what you're working on.

Why it works: Real connections happen when you're not trying to "network", you're just being present and curious.

📝 2. Follow Up Like a Human

After meeting someone professionally, send a short message within 48 hours. Remind them who you are, mention something specific from your conversation, and thank them for their time or advice.

Example:

"Hi Jordan, it was great meeting you at the NextSteps gala. I really appreciated hearing about your early days in tech, thank you for encouraging me to stay curious. I'd love to stay in touch!"

Why it works: Polite, low-pressure follow-ups build long-term goodwill and open doors over time.

📅 3. Stay in Touch Without Being Weird

Put a reminder in your calendar to check in with a connection every two to three months. Share a quick update, article, or question related to their field or your shared interests.

Why it works: Most people *don't* do this. So, when you do, you'll stand out as someone who's thoughtful, proactive, and worth remembering.

CHAPTER 20: THE TEAMMATE WHO CHANGED THE VIBE

"Energy is contagious, make yours worth catching."

University of Houston – Early Fall

The Learning Commons buzzed with scattered footsteps, low conversations, and the ever-present hum of laptops. Outside, the Houston heat clung to the windows like plastic wrap. Inside, Nina adjusted her seat at the far corner of a group study table, trying not to feel the full weight of awkward silence.

It was day one of their entrepreneurship class project, and the vibe was ... not great.

She glanced at her team. Logan stared into his laptop like it had personally betrayed him. Anika scrolled on her phone with AirPods in. Terrell drummed his fingers, clearly ready to leave. No one had even said *hi*.

Their assignment? Develop and pitch a socially conscious startup idea in six weeks. But judging by the energy in the room, they'd be lucky to get a group chat going.

Nina shifted in her seat, chewing her lip.

She'd worked on plenty of teams before through student orgs, summer jobs, and a surprisingly intense high school debate team. She wasn't always the smartest in the room, or the loudest. But

one thing had always been true: people worked better when they *wanted* to show up.

Right now, no one did.

The Decision to Shift the Mood

She thought about walking out and letting the project limp along. No one would blame her. But something nudged her: *If the mood's bad, make it better.*

She looked up.

"Hey," she said, her voice steady but casual. "We all seem tired. Want to just take five minutes to chill before we dive in? I brought snacks, Houston survival kit: Takis, trail mix, and cold-brew pouches."

Terrell raised an eyebrow. "Cold brew?"

"You know," she said, pulling it from her tote. "The fuel of ideas."

For the first time, someone chuckled.

They took the break.

They talked, not about the project, but about the worst Houston humidity stories and who had the best tacos on campus. Nina kept things light, asked a few open-ended questions, and stayed genuinely curious.

CHAPTER 20: THE TEAMMATE WHO CHANGED THE VIBE

After 10 minutes, Anika unplugged her AirPods.

"So... should we start?"

The Slow Shift

The next meeting, Nina brought a whiteboard and scribbled "Bad Ideas First" in big letters. "Let's get the weird ones out before we judge them," she grinned.

Logan suggested a micro-loan app for student entrepreneurs. It was messy. Half-baked. But Nina nodded. "That's something. Let's follow it."

Week by week, something shifted.

Logan stopped acting like he was forced to be there. Terrell started showing up early. Anika created a killer wireframe for the prototype.

Nina wasn't leading in the traditional sense. She didn't boss anyone around. But she showed up early. She came prepared. She celebrated small wins and defused the awkward silences.

And it mattered.

Presentation Day

Their startup pitch, CampusFund, a platform connecting students to short-term, interest-free funding for campus initiatives, wasn't perfect. But it was solid. Cohesive. Passionate.

After their presentation, the professor said, "You're the only team that seemed like you actually *liked* working together."

Nina smiled.

Later That Week

They grabbed tacos at a spot just off-campus to celebrate.

Logan raised his horchata. "Real talk, Nina, you changed this team."

Nina shrugged. "All I did was bring snacks."

Anika smirked. "And optimism. Which honestly might've been more effective."

Skill: Positive Attitude

- ☑ **Energy is contagious; your tone can set the tone.**

- ☑ **Positivity doesn't mean fake cheer. It means choosing solutions over complaints.**

- ☑ **Group projects, workplaces, and relationships thrive when someone believes in the outcome. Be that someone.**

∼

Practice the Skill: Positive Attitude

1. Be the Thermostat, Not the Thermometer

Next time you're in a group setting–class, work, a club–notice the emotional tone. Instead of reflecting it, *reset* it. Use simple energy shifts: greet people warmly, bring light humor, acknowledge stress but offer encouragement.

Why it works: People subconsciously sync with emotional leaders. Set a tone of hope and ease, and others often follow.

2. Reframe Before You React

When something frustrating happens (e.g., a teammate slacks, plans change, tech fails), pause before venting. Try a quick reframe:

> Instead of: "This is a disaster," try: "This is a curveball we can catch."

> Instead of: "No one cares," try: "What can I do to invite them in?"

Why it works: Positivity isn't about pretending everything's fine; it's about choosing a mindset that moves things forward.

💬 3. Use Encouragement as a Tool, Not a Fluff

Once per group meeting or day, call out something specific someone did well:

> "That example you used really grounded the idea."

> "Your slide design gave the pitch a clean edge."

> "I appreciate you stepping in when things got off track."

Why it works: Positivity builds trust. When people feel seen, they show up more fully, and the work improves.

CHAPTER 21: THE CONTACT THEY ALMOST IGNORED

"Networking isn't collecting contacts, it's cultivating connections."

San Francisco, California – Catalyst Conference, Moscone Center

Lucas leaned against a tall window at the Moscone Center, watching the tide of entrepreneur's buzz between booths. Lanyards tangled. Jargon flew. LED banners flashed startup names like Nebula Box and CryptoMech. Lucas adjusted his name tag and exhaled. These things always made him feel like a poser.

A senior at San Francisco State University, Lucas had a real reason to be here. He wanted to help small, under-resourced businesses like his mom's bakery in the Mission. But surrounded by people chasing unicorns and Series A rounds, he felt like he didn't belong.

Still, he'd promised himself he'd stay for at least an hour.

Out of the corner of his eye, he noticed a man adjusting a Blue Bottle Coffee sign at the snack station. Button-down shirt. Relaxed energy. No badge. He nodded politely at Lucas, who nodded back then returned to his phone.

The Conversation That Shifted His Perspective

About thirty minutes later, the same man approached Lucas with two paper cups in hand.

"Mind if I join you?"

Lucas blinked. "Sure."

"I'm Sam," the man said. "You look like you're keeping a safe distance from the pitch parade."

Lucas laughed awkwardly. "Is it that obvious?"

"Just enough," Sam replied. "These events can feel ... performative. But the best connections usually happen offstage."

"I'm Lucas," he said. "Business major at SFSU. I came hoping to meet people, but honestly? I'm not great at this whole networking thing."

"Maybe that's because you're trying to do it someone else's way," Sam said. "Why are you here, really?"

Lucas hesitated, then shrugged. "My mom owns a bakery back in the Mission. I've watched her struggle–rising costs, no marketing help, no support. I want to help small businesses like hers. But most people here seem laser-focused on apps and exits."

Sam smiled. "You'd be surprised how rare your kind of clarity is. Real impact starts with real stories."

CHAPTER 21: THE CONTACT THEY ALMOST IGNORED

Lucas looked around at the bustling conference doubtfully. "It feels like I'm in the wrong place with these goals."

"There's *only* room if people like you make it," Sam replied. "I started Prism Ventures for that exact reason. To back local entrepreneurs with heart. We don't invest in apps. We invest in people."

A New Way to Network

Later, Lucas learned that Sam wasn't just a nice guy with coffee. He was Samuel Carter, founder of Prism Ventures, a community-focused investment firm known for supporting local businesses.

Lucas had nearly ignored one of the most influential people at the conference, just because he didn't look the part.

Over the next few weeks, Lucas took Sam's words to heart. He stopped rehearsing pitches and started building conversations. He visited small businesses in the Mission and SoMa, asking owners about their pain points, marketing gaps, loan access, and staffing challenges.

He met Ana, who ran a cozy bookstore in a converted garage. "We do not have many sales," she said. "Not many people come by."

Instead of offering unsolicited advice, Lucas asked questions. Took notes. Listened.

Then he wrote to Sam.

Turning Connection into Action

Lucas proposed a pilot program: a series of workshops pairing business students with small business owners to co-create practical growth plans. Nothing fancy, just help that met people where they were.

Sam replied within the day: "Let's talk. This is exactly the kind of thing we need more of."

They met again at Prism's SoMa office, which smelled like fresh eucalyptus and espresso. Sam shared his own story, how he'd started with nothing but a laptop and an idea after being overlooked by every firm in town.

"I know what it's like to not fit the mold," Sam said. "You don't need polish to lead. You need purpose."

Lucas smiled. "And people willing to believe in it."

Sam nodded. "Start small. Start local. The rest will follow."

Overcoming Resistance

Organizing the first workshop wasn't easy. A few business owners ghosted him. Some politely declined. Others were skeptical.

Lucas had moments where he almost gave up.

But Ana signed up. She brought her stubborn hope and a spiral notebook filled with scribbled ideas. With help from Lucas and a few classmates, she launched her first online book sale for local college students. Orders trickled in. Then poured.

By the third workshop, four more businesses had signed up. Word was spreading.

Full Circle

Months later, Lucas stood backstage at the Moscone Center, again. Only this time, he wasn't a bystander.

He was standing next to Sam, prepping to co-present on grassroots business acceleration.

CHAPTER 21: THE CONTACT THEY ALMOST IGNORED

Sam turned to him. "You ready?"

Lucas looked out at the crowd. "Yeah," he said. "But this time, I'm not here to impress anyone. I'm here to share what's possible."

He walked onstage, scanned the crowd, and spotted Ana in the front row.

"When I first came to this conference," Lucas began, "I thought networking was about selling yourself. But someone taught me it's really about showing up with honesty, curiosity, and care. That's how real relationships start. And that's how real change happens."

The room went still.

Then came the applause.

And this time, it felt real.

Skill:
Meaningful Networking & Influence

✅ **Authentic connections build lasting influence; transactional networking rarely does.**

✅ **Real networking starts with listening, not asking. Contributing, not performing.**

✅ **When you lead with care, people remember *how* you showed up, not just what you said.**

～

Practice the Skill: Meaningful Networking & Influence

1. "No-Ask" Conversation

Reach out to someone in your network—a professor, club advisor, or local business owner—and request a short conversation just to learn more about their story or work. Ask no favors. Just listen and learn.

Why it works: The most impactful networking is rooted in genuine curiosity, not immediate gain. People remember the ones who made them feel heard.

2. Craft a Thoughtful Follow-Up

After attending an event or meeting someone new, follow up within 48 hours. In your message, include one specific detail from your conversation that stood out and thank them for their time or insight.

Why it works: Specificity signals sincerity. It shows you weren't just collecting a contact; you were connecting with a person.

3. Build a Relationship Tracker

Create a simple spreadsheet or notebook to keep track of people you've met, how you met them, what you learned from them, and when you last followed up.

Why it works: Professional networks grow over time, not all at once. This helps you nurture authentic connections without letting them fade.

CHAPTER 22: THE COMPLAINT SHE DIDN'T MAKE

"Anyone can point out problems; leaders suggest solutions."

Fairfax, Virginia – George Mason University, Johnson Center Café

Haley sat by the wide window of the Johnson Center Café, spring sun warming her shoulders as the energy of campus buzzed around her. Students laughed over iced lattes and swapped weekend plans, but Haley's stomach churned with nerves.

She glanced down at her planner then at the Patriot Activities Council agenda for tonight's emergency meeting. The headliner for PatriotFest, the university's biggest spring event, had just canceled due to a scheduling mix-up.

Haley had helped plan every detail. She remembered watching her older sister Emily lead the event years ago and how inspired she'd been. This was her chance to carry on that tradition. And now? Chaos.

She could already picture the meeting: complaints, finger-pointing, and pressure. But then a voice echoed in her mind, her mom's calm, steady reminder from childhood:

If you're going to point out a problem, bring a solution too.

Haley sat up straighter and opened her laptop.

The Shift in Mindset

Instead of rehearsing what had gone wrong, Haley began researching local bands around Arlington and Alexandria. She sent DMs to several of them on Instagram, explaining the last-minute opportunity.

One response came within ten minutes: Pink Skyline, a rising indie-rock band known at a few D.C.-area colleges, was available and excited. Haley's shoulders relaxed for the first time all day.

Just in case, she drafted backup plans too: a student open mic featuring campus talent or a DJ-led dance party by WGMU Radio. Not perfect, but better than nothing.

Turning the Room

That evening, the student union conference room felt more like a pressure cooker. The fluorescent lights buzzed. The vibe? Frustration.

Jenna, the council president, was already responding to anxious voices.

"This could tank the whole thing," someone said. "We've sunk so much money already."

Haley, heart pounding, raised her hand. Jenna's eyes met hers. "Haley?"

"I know this is overwhelming," she began. "But I reached out to some local bands. One of them, Pink Skyline, is free, and they're willing to work with our budget. I also have a few backup ideas if that doesn't work."

The room quieted. Even Marcus, the most skeptical member, looked intrigued.

Jenna paused, then nodded. "Okay. Let's explore it."

And just like that, the room's energy shifted, from panic to problem-solving.

The Quad, Reimagined

The following Friday, the grassy campus Quad came alive. Colorful lights shimmered across the crowd. Students swayed and sang along as Pink Skyline played under the stars.

Haley stood near the sound booth, watching everything unfold. Her nerves had been replaced by a quiet pride. Jenna found her mid-show and squeezed her arm.

"You didn't just fix the problem," she said. "You saved the spirit of this event."

Haley smiled. "I almost just joined the complaints. But then I remembered what my mom used to say."

Jenna raised an eyebrow. "Let me guess, bring solutions?"

Haley laughed. "Exactly."

The Message That Mattered Most

The following Monday, back in the same café, Haley opened her inbox. A message from Jenna was waiting.

Subject: Next Year

> Haley,
>
> I just wanted to thank you again. Everyone saw how you handled that mess with calm, creative leadership. Next year, I'd love for you to apply to lead the council. You've got the mindset we need.

Haley reread the message twice. Then she clicked reply.

> Count me in.

Skill:
Proactively Offering Solutions

☑ Leaders don't just point out problems, they propose paths forward.

☑ Offering even imperfect ideas earns trust and shifts the tone.

☑ Positive problem-solving is noticed and remembered.

∼

Practice the Skill: Proactively Offering Solutions

🧠 1. Two-for-One Rule

Whenever you identify a problem at school, work, or in a group, challenge yourself to bring at least two possible solutions.

Why it works: It trains your brain to think like a leader and shows others that you're invested in moving forward, not just pointing fingers.

👤 2. Reframe the Frustration

Next time you're tempted to say, "This isn't going to work," try saying, "What if we tried this instead?" or "Here's another way we could approach it."

Why it works: Reframing turns negativity into momentum, and people are more likely to listen when you bring options, not obstacles.

📖 3. Reflect on a Win

Think back to a time when you helped solve a problem, big or small. What did you suggest? How did it help the group? Write it down and note how people responded.

Why it works: Celebrating past solution moments builds confidence and reminds you that progress often starts with one idea.

CHAPTER 23: THE JOG THAT OPENED A DOOR

*"Every connection is a door.
You never know which one will open, so show up ready."*

Southern California – San Diego State University

Michele didn't consider herself a natural networker. She wasn't shy, but she wasn't the type to drop business cards like confetti or dominate career fairs. She was an urban planning student at San Diego State University passionate about interiors, architecture, and real estate.

"I love how space makes people feel," she once told her advisor. "It's not just about furniture. It's about energy."

So, when she saw a flyer for a guest presentation by the San Diego Realtors Association taped to the bulletin board outside the design building, her curiosity lit up. She registered, showed up early, took notes, and stayed after to thank the speaker Lynn Dawson, the association's outreach director.

"Thanks for such an insightful presentation," Michele said, smiling. "I'm studying design, but I'm really drawn to real estate. I'd love to learn more, are there any internship opportunities you'd recommend?"

Lynn blinked, pleasantly surprised. "That's a great question. Connect with me. I'd be happy to stay in touch."

She handed Michele her card. No promises. Just a door left slightly open.

That evening, Michele followed up with a short email:

> Thank you again for your time today. I appreciated how you broke down the local housing trends. If any volunteer or learning opportunities open up, I'd love to be considered.

Two months passed.

Then, on a Tuesday afternoon, Michele received an email from Lynn:

> Hi Michele, we're hosting a private networking mixer for real estate professionals next week. Would you like to attend as my guest? I think you'd get a lot out of it.

She was stunned and said yes immediately.

The Mixer in Mission Hills

The event was held in a restored craftsman home turned staging showroom in Mission Hills. Realtors, brokers, stagers, and interior designers sipped sparkling water near stone fireplaces, chatting beneath Edison bulbs.

Michele felt a familiar nervous flutter. What if she didn't belong?

But she remembered what her mentor once said: *You don't need to be the expert. You just need to be curious.*

So, she listened, asked thoughtful questions, and introduced herself with honesty.

"I'm a design student at SDSU, and I'm really interested in learning how design intersects with real estate. Would you mind if we connected so I could learn from your journey?"

Not everyone said yes. But many did.

That night, Michele sent personalized thank-you emails to everyone she met.

The Jog That Changed Everything

Three weeks later, on a Sunday morning jog through North Park, Michele saw a woman struggling to pull a large sandwich board sign from the trunk of her SUV.

"Need a hand?" Michele asked, slowing down.

"Oh, thank you! That would be amazing," the woman said, laughing. "This thing always gets stuck."

Michele helped her gently wrangle the sign out. As the woman turned to thank her again, she paused. "Wait ... I know you. You're Michele, right? From the event last month?"

Michele blinked. "Yes! I'm surprised you remember."

"I never forget someone who follows up with sincerity," the woman said. "I'm Claire. I'm hosting an open house down the block. Want to walk with me?"

As they walked, Claire asked Michele about school, design, and her plans after graduation. Then she said something unexpected.

"You know, the sellers of this property run a boutique architecture firm in downtown San Diego. They're always looking for interns with a good eye and a good attitude. Can I pass your name along?"

Michele tried not to beam. "I'd really appreciate that."

Three Weeks Later

Michele walked into the lobby of Sea Front Studio, the architecture firm Claire had mentioned. The space was filled with natural light and soft jazz, the walls lined with mood boards and renderings of upcoming projects.

She was there for an interview.

The hiring manager smiled and said, "Claire spoke very highly of you. She said you weren't just curious; you were kind."

Skill: Networking

☑ Networking doesn't require status, it requires presence.

☑ Ask good questions, be genuinely curious, and always follow up with grace.

☑ You never know who's watching or where a connection might lead. Be consistent in how you show up.

Practice the Skill: Networking

1. Start with Curiosity, Not a Pitch

Instead of leading with what you want, begin by showing genuine interest in someone else's work. Ask thoughtful questions like, "How did you get started in this field?" or "What do you love most about your work?"

Why it works: People remember curiosity. It builds connection without pressure.

2. Follow Up Within 24 Hours

After the event, send a short, kind message (email or text if you have it) to the people you have met. Include in your message:

What you appreciated about your conversation

A thank-you

An invitation to stay in touch

Example:

"Hi Claire, it was such a pleasure meeting you at the event yesterday. I really enjoyed hearing about your work in design and real estate, your story inspired me. I'd love to stay connected and learn more when the time is right."

Why it works: A timely follow-up shows you're intentional, not forgettable.

3. Keep the Loop Open, Without Overdoing It

Once you've connected, check in every few months with a quick update, a thoughtful question, or something you've learned. Don't ask for anything right away, just share your progress and appreciation.

Example:

"Hi Lynn, I wanted to thank you again for inviting me to the spring mixer. I just wrapped up my semester and started a new design project I'd love to tell you about sometime!"

Why it works: Staying on someone's radar in a respectful way builds long-term professional relationships, without feeling transactional.

CHAPTER 24:
THE LETTERS THAT FOUND THEIR TRAIN

*"You waited, you learned, you boarded.
Now turn around and help someone else step forward."*

The skyline shimmered through the glass. Dax leaned back in his chair on the 38th floor, the ink on the contract still drying beside him.

$568 million.

The number glowed at the top of the page, the kind of deal that landed people on magazine covers. His firm had just closed a multi-year partnership between a national sustainability startup and a legacy logistics company, something that would change how goods moved across the U.S.

Yet Dax wasn't thinking about the money.

He was thinking about a train.

Outside, the station pulsed with its usual midday rhythm. He could just make out the silver glint of a commuter train pulling in, passengers hurrying across the platform below.

He remembered standing there once–young, uncertain, invisible–holding a leather portfolio no one asked to see. He remembered the station keeper. The cap. The voice. The lesson: *"Each of them carries a story that earned them a place on the train."*

At the time, Dax didn't understand what that meant. Now he did.

What He Carried

Success didn't come all at once. It came in fragments, humbling team projects, feedback that cut deep, missed emails, moments when he wanted to disappear. But the lessons? They came loud and clear, each one tethered to a face, a chapter, a turning point.

He thought of Jordan reading her poem near a food truck in Bushwick.

Karina, asking the question that changed her project group's entire approach.

Zaria, taking ownership for a mistake that nearly derailed a campaign.

He hadn't just learned from his own path.

He had learned from theirs.

And now, he was ready to pass it on.

The First Letter

It started with a talk he gave at a local college.

The students were quiet at first, polite, cautious. But during Q&A, a junior in the front row asked a question that pierced straight through him.

CHAPTER 24: THE LETTERS THAT FOUND THEIR TRAIN

"How did you know when it was your turn to board the train?"

Dax paused. Looked at the students. Saw himself.

"I didn't," he finally said. "I just stopped waiting for someone to announce it."

That night, he wrote a letter to his 19-year-old self. Not a motivational speech. Just the kind of honesty he wished he'd had.

He posted it on social media with the hashtag

#letterstomyyoungself_Dax

He expected a few likes.

He got thousands.

What It Became

Letters poured in.

From baristas. From analysts. From early-career nurses and burnt-out creatives. From people who had made it or were still trying to. Each one a small offering:

"I wish someone had told me it's okay to outgrow people who can't grow with you."

"No one teaches you how to speak up in meetings, you have to learn by trembling through it."

"You're allowed to not have it all figured out. Just don't stop showing up."

Dax printed them. Hung them on the wall of the team's shared workspace. A growing constellation of truths.

Eventually, he compiled them into a book. He wrote the introduction himself. Not as a CEO but as someone who remembered what it felt like to knock without an answer.

The Train Metaphor, Rewritten

In the book's final chapter, he wrote:

"Trains don't wait for perfect résumés. They stop for people who've done the invisible work: learning to listen, ask, adapt, show up, take ownership.

Each letter in this book is a kind of boarding pass, one someone earned the hard way. And now they're offering it to you."

A Letter from Dax

To My 19-Year-Old Self

Subject: You Are Not Invisible

> You're doing everything you were told.
> You're working hard. Polishing your résumé. Following the steps. And still, the doors won't open.
>
> It's not because you're unworthy.
> It's because no one taught you the secret curriculum.
>
> How to be visible.
> How to ask for help.
>
> How to take feedback without unraveling.
> How to listen like a leader.
>
> How to network.
> How to stand your ground and still stay kind.

CHAPTER 24: THE LETTERS THAT FOUND THEIR TRAIN

I know you're tired of being the one left behind.
But hear me now: *You are not behind. You are becoming.*

Keep learning. Keep stepping forward. Even when no one calls your name.

Your train is coming.

Dax

A Letter from Karina

To the Girl Who Just Bombed the Quiz

Subject: You're Not Bad at This

I know it feels like a wall.

But it's not a wall. It's a slope. And you're still climbing.

You don't need to "get it" right away. You just need to believe that you can.

Find your pace. Ask the question. Take the pause. Rewrite your notes in your own language. You're not behind; you're just early in your own process.

I didn't believe I could get through that class either.

Until I did.

And you will, too.

Karina

Full Circle

Months later, Dax was waiting at the station, this time for a train he was actually boarding. A college student approached him timidly, holding a copy of his book.

The corners were dog-eared. Lines highlighted. Sticky notes spilling from the sides.

"You're … Dax, right?"

He smiled. "Yeah."

The student held up the book. "That part about how asking questions makes you visible? That helped me stay in my engineering program. I almost dropped out."

Dax's throat tightened.

"That's the only reason I'm even on this platform today."

He nodded, eyes soft.

"Then it was worth writing."

The train doors opened.

And this time, they both stepped on.

I Would Love to Hear from You!

Thank you so much for reading this book. It means the world to me. If you found it helpful, inspiring, or just enjoyable, would you take a moment to leave an honest review? Your feedback not only helps others but also keeps me motivated to create more valuable content for you.

Here's how you can leave a review:

Visit your Amazon Orders page, find this book, and click "Write a Product Review."

Thank you for your support!

∼

PERSONAL SKILLS ASSESSMENT

From Invisible to Valuable: Skills for Career Success

INTRODUCTION

This assessment will help you identify your current strengths and areas for growth across the essential career skills covered in "From Invisible to Valuable." Rate yourself honestly. This is your personal roadmap to professional development.

SKILLS SELF-EVALUATION

Rating Scale: 1 = Needs significant development; 2 = Basic awareness but limited application; 3 = Developing competency; 4 = Strong application in most situations; 5 = Exceptional strength, can teach others.

H – High, M – Medium, L – Low

COMMUNICATION SKILLS

Skill	Rating (1-5)	Priority for Growth (H/M/L)
Speaking with Clarity & Courage		
Effective Communication		
Asking Questions		
Speaking Up in Groups		
Listening to Understand		

PROFESSIONAL PRESENCE

Skill	Rating (1-5)	Priority for Growth (H/M/L)
Personal Branding		
Punctuality		
Professionalism		
Poise		
Positive Attitude		

PERSONAL EFFECTIVENESS

Skill	Rating (1-5)	Priority for Growth (H/M/L)
Time Management		
Growth Mindset		
Receiving Feedback		
Self-Awareness		

INTERPERSONAL SKILLS

Skill	Rating (1-5)	Priority for Growth (H/M/L)
Collaboration		
Empathy		
Networking		
Integrity		
Gratitude & Follow-Through		

LEADERSHIP QUALITIES

Skill	Rating (1-5)	Priority for Growth (H/M/L)
Accountability		
Adaptability		
Problem Solving		
Setting the Tone		

DEVELOPMENT PRIORITIES

Based on your assessment, identify your:

Top 3 Strengths:

1. _____

2. _____

3. _____

Top 3 Growth Areas:

1. _____

2. _____

3. _____

MONTHLY PROGRESS TRACKER

Month: _____

REFLECTION QUESTIONS

After completing this assessment, ask yourself:

1. What patterns did you notice in your skill evaluation?

2. How do your self-identified strengths align with feedback you've received from others?

3. Which skill gaps might be holding you back from current goals?

4. Which skill development would create the greatest immediate impact in your life?

5. Who could support or mentor you in developing your priority skills?

COMMITMENT

This month I commit to developing these 2 professional skills because:

_____

_____

_____

_____

_____

_____

_____

My first action steps will be:

_____

_____

_____

_____

_____

Date: _____ Signature: _____

This Personal Skills Assessment is a companion resource to *From Invisible to Valuable: Skills for Career Success* by Doron Noyman

You can download a PDF version of this worksheet and other resources at: https://stan.store/DoronNoyman

Notes

Notes

Notes

Notes

Made in the USA
Coppell, TX
22 July 2025